The Saga of the Buffalo

The Saga of

CY MARTIN

the Buffalo

Hart Publishing Company, Inc., New York

Contents

The Saga of the Buffalo

George Catlin painting of Plains Indians stalking a buffalo stuck in a snowdrift.

Introduction

*T*oday, the word "buffalo" may merely call to mind a hunchbacked cow on a nickel, or the name of a city in New York State, but there was a time when the entire future of western America hinged on whether there were to be buffalo west of the Mississippi. In fact, along about 1870, Congress seriously debated whether the United States—for all its resources —could wrest the West away from the Indians, or whether it would be better to give the idea up as hopeless. The key to the situation was the curly cow that roamed the plains—the buffalo.

More than a million Americans toiled their way slowly and painfully over the prairies before railroads crossed the continent. For half a century, America's greatest cattle herd served those million people, and served them royally. The buffalo fed them with juicy fresh meat, covered them with rich robes, supplied them with fuel, showed them the way to the water holes, and marked the fords where their covered wagons could cross.

The American *Bison* was—and is—the biggest animal on the North American continent. A full-grown bull stands about six feet at the shoulder and is, on the average, from ten to twelve feet long, tail included. His average weight is eighteen hundred pounds; but animals weighing as much as twenty-four hundred pounds have been recorded in the history books.

The horns are not especially long, but the breadth of the savage crown between them is impressive. With those stout horns, a bull could rip the rope-tough prairie sod to make himself a dust wallow, toss a whole wolf pack, disembowel a horse—even carry the horse and rider aloft for a hundred yards before finally hurling them to the ground. A cow defending her calf is one of the world's most ferocious animals. As for a herd of buffalo on the move, no creature ever stood its ground to argue with a stampede and lived more than sixty seconds.

Before the white man came, the bison was the most numerous of all the earth's big land mammals. Naturalists differ in their estimates of the total number, but no one suggests there were less than 50 million. The early explorers and cowboys could not find words to

Mandan bull dancer.

describe the great hordes of these monarchs of the prairies. In the era of the steamboat, traffic on the Missouri River was stopped for days by buffalo herds swimming the stream.

It was the greatest supply of fresh meat the Creator ever bestowed on a lucky country. But, owing to man's greed and waste, less than one-third of the buffalo slaughtered were ever used for anything. Certain food faddists on the prairie killed the bison only for their delicious tongues, then left the remains to wolves. For years buffalo were killed only for the hides. Pioneers butchered them to fatten their hogs, and millions were slain simply to clear them off the fertile prairie land.

By 1810, the bison were pushed over the Mississippi, and there was no trace of them in the eastern forests; only the trails they had made walking in single file remained. Daniel Boone's Wilderness Road followed, in large part, a buffalo path from Tennessee, through the Cumberland Gap to the salt licks of Kentucky. Many a modern city stands where it is today because the American bison beat an ancient trail to the site.

The toll of doom came for the plains herds with the laying of the transcontinental railway. The buffalo did not take this invasion sitting down. He met it head on! He pushed down the new telegraph poles; he stood on the railroad tracks and stopped the trains. He charged between the cars, broke the couplings, overturned boxcars.

The Kansas Pacific Railroad hired Colonel William Cody, at the fancy figure of five hundred dollars a month, to clear the snorting brutes from the railroad right-of-way. Cody, with his gang of exterminators, not only killed off the herds, but also supplied the construction crews with fresh fancy cuts of meat daily.

Confronted with such major attacks, the buffalo unknowingly faced their destiny. The great beasts just had to yield before the white man. The pioneer's farms, his fences, cattle, sheep, and crops could not share the prairie with these ferocious curly cows. In 1865, the Santa Fe's "Buffalo" Jones declared flatly there remained only 15 million bison. Yet, in that year alone over 1 million were slaughtered. Half of the remainder were gone by 1872, at the peak of the buffalo kill. In 1883, Montana's biggest herd of over ten thousand animals was exterminated in just a few days. Sharpshooters guarded every water hole during the burning summer hours and by firelight at night. When the thirst-maddened brutes charged to get water, not a single animal escaped.

George Catlin painting of Pawnee warrior Buffalo Bull.

Much of the slaughter was for the sake of the hides alone, which soared in price as they decreased in quantity. These dry hides were heaped beside the railroad in piles as high as Kansas haystacks, for mile after mile. Toward the very end, the poor creature was made the target of an expensive sport. It became fashionable for wealthy hunters of big game and titled visitors to "kill the last buffalo." The Grand Duke Alexis of Russia had a hunt arranged by General Sheridan, who enlisted General Custer, Colonel Cody, a pack of Indian scouts, and a troop of U. S. Cavalry to round up some of the lonely animals. After the hunt, a buffalo barbecue was held with champagne flowing freely.

Soon, where once sovereign herds thundered, only bleached bones remained. Acre after acre of bones! Contemporary photographs show that the plains were white with them as far as the eye could see. And, even in this skeleton form, the buffalo helped the western pioneer. The bones—with their high market value for use in sugar refining and as fertilizer—helped many an early settler pay his first land fee. He sold the buffalo bones he cleared off his claim at the nearest railroad siding.

The buffalo gave light and warmth wherever he had passed. For years after the herds vanished, travelers across the treeless plains found a ready hot fuel in the buffalo chips. Over campfires made with such fuel many a heartening meal was cooked and many a tall tale spun. Even when the chips were gone, prairie settlers could still trace their way to the water holes because the buffalo paths, having for ages been fertilized by the droppings of the great animals, were always marked by the growth of taller, greener grass.

The prairie sod was broken and fenced. The steam cars crisscrossed the plains on their iron rails. Exiled, hunted, the last few buffalo were facing total extinction. Only a few men perceived that an important part of our American heritage would be gone when the last of the bison were dead.

Walking Coyote, a Pend d'Oreille Indian, was the vanishing buffalo's first friend. He caught two male and two female calves, and from that meager beginning, grew the great Allard-Pancho and Conrad herds of Montana. In the Texas Panhandle, Colonel Charles Goodnight, to please his wife, saved a few wild calves by luring them home to the protection of his ranch.

The American Bison Society, founded in 1905 by Theodore Roosevelt, raised fifty thousand dollars to create the great Montana National Bison Range. Today, there are herds in Nebraska, Oklahoma, South Dakota, and Yellowstone Park. The buffalo population of the United States now totals over six thousand, and there are presently more buffalo calves coming into the world than there is range land to accommodate them. Most of the surplus goes to the Indians. This is very fitting, for to the Indian the buffalo is a creature of divine origin, a gift of the Great Spirit. He is an ancient figure in their religious ceremonies.

To any American, the buffalo should be a prized fellow citizen, and the memory of his former greatness should quicken our hearts as long as the bunchgrass grows out west.

This, then, is the story of "Old Man Buffalo," his friends, enemies, and killers. He played a major role in the opening of the great American West. Without the buffalo, railroads would have failed; homesteaders would have frozen and starved. Truly, "Our Father, the Buffalo" was the symbol of the growth of the western United States.

This sketch is believed to be the earliest European representation of the buffalo. It first appeared in HISTORIA GENERAL DE LAS INDIAS, *published by Francisco Lopez de Gomara in mid-16th century.*

Life of the Shaggy Beast

In **1851,** there were more buffalo in the United States than there were people. Yet, within a period of less than fifty years, this unique animal nearly became extinct. Various estimates of the number of buffalo in 1851 vary from 75 million to over 100 million. However, in 1900 there were less than twenty-five hundred animals in the various zoological gardens throughout the U. S. A.

Where, indeed how, did the buffalo—an animal hardy enough to surmount the hazards of thousands of years—go?

The buffalo was destroyed by man. Man was his only real enemy, for the buffalo was adapted perfectly to the Great Plains of our West.

What of the myriad buffalo herds that inhabited this same area before the coming of the white man?

With no airplanes to drop food to the beasts when they were snowbound, and no one to care if they froze to death, how did they manage? They thrived exceedingly well and multiplied unbelievably, for they were bred of the blizzard and were one with all of Nature's moods. Of all the big game that has roamed the earth within recorded history, no species has ever equaled in number the animals that were to become known as *Bison americanus* or the buffalo.

How did they manage to increase so tremendously on the very same plains where the white man's cattle drifted before the storms and died by the thousands? Let's go back in time and take a look at the Great Plains of the U.S.A.

The life of the buffalo, even without man's intervention, was hardly placid. Wolves lurked on the fringe of each herd, alert for every chance at prey; coyotes attacked the weak and disabled. Frequently, the animals were killed by lightning from a prairie thunderstorm. At times, the buffalo themselves would kill each other in a mad stampede.

But, no, these natural dangers did not effectively reduce the total population of the buffalo. The slaughter began when the white man first set foot on these shores. The Indians, of course, made little dent in the total bison population. But when, after the year 1500, the white explorers came and started to prowl around, how the story changed!

Curiously enough, the first European to lay eyes on a buffalo saw it in a menagerie. This man was Cortez, the Spanish conqueror of Mexico, and the menagerie was the one the famous Aztec emperor, Montezuma, had assembled. The Spaniards were quite startled by this new type of "cow." One of them wrote learnedly how it was a "composite of several and divers animals," since it had the lion's mane, flanks, and tufted tail; the goat's beard; the camel's hump; and the cow's hooves. Way back in 1533, Cabeza de Vaca wrote about the "Indian cattle" he had seen during his travels in Texas. His stories of the vast numbers of buffalo were discounted as the tales of just another teller of tall stories.

Cabeza de Vaca described the buffalo by saying:

Cattle come as far as here. Three times have I seen them and eaten of their meat. . . To my judgment the flesh is finer and fatter than that of this country [Spain]. Of the skins of those not full grown the Indians make blankets, and of the larger they make shoes and bucklers. They come as far as the seacoast of Florida, from a northerly direction, ranging through a tract of more than four hundred leagues; and throughout the whole region over which they run, the people who inhabit near, descend and live upon them, distributing a great many hides into the interior country.

People did not take de Vaca seriously until 1636, when eyewitness accounts became more common.

But the Spaniards were in for a greater surprise. When they first saw the buffalo on his native prairie, never in their lives had they ever come upon such an enormous concentration of shaggy animals. One little band of explorers made a report of their first discovery. They were first attracted, they said, by a peculiar reddish dust haze beyond a range of low hills. Climbing a hill to investigate, they were startled by the sight of a vast "Brown Sea," a restless, moving mass of animals that stretched as far as the eye could see—to the very horizon itself. Buffalo, hundreds of thousands of them, and that was only the beginning. The explorers pushed onward for weeks and weeks, and never once lost sight of the mass of animals. They sent glowing accounts back to Spain, declaring the new "cattle" to be as "plentiful as the fish in the sea," and raved over the excellence of the fresh meat.

Then, having proved that the new land had a treasure well worth the price of admission, the explorers turned on the buffalo and began to slaughter them with almost insane enthusiasm. Apparently this was just for the fun of it. The buffalo were as easy to shoot as carp in a barrel, even for Spaniards carrying such clumsy, primitive firearms as the harquebus and the matchlock musket. These big weapons—each as awkward as a bazooka—were so heavy that two men were needed to hold, aim, and fire one of them. Reloading was a slow and major operation. But these minor drawbacks did not matter in buffalo shooting. The curly cows were jammed shoulder to shoulder right in front of them, and if they missed one they were bound to hit another.

Even so, shooting the heavy weapons was tiring sport. So, one daring cavalier made a thrust at a buffalo with his pike (a spear carried by European soldiers) and was surprised to see it fall over dead. From then on, the Conquistadors carried on the slaughter with renewed zest. This was the early beginning of a campaign of cruelty and waste that was not to end until nearly the last buffalo on the continent was left dead on the plains.

When the Lewis and Clark expedition, progressing up the Missouri, passed the mouth of the Judith River, Captain Lewis wrote in his *Journal:*

> *Today we passed on the Stard. side the remains of a vast many mangled carcases of Buffalow which had been driven over a precipice of 120 feet by the Indian and perished; the water appeared to have washed away a part of this immence pile of slaughter and still their remained the fragments of at least a hundred carcases . . . they created a most horrid stench. in this manner the Indians of the Missouri distroy vast herds of buffaloe at a stroke; . . . for this purpose one of the most*

active and fleet young men is scelected and disguised in a robe of buffaloe skin, having also the skin of the buffaloe's head with the years and horns fastened on his head in form of a cap, thus caparisoned he places himself at a convenient distance between a herd of buffaloe and a precipice proper for the purpose, which happens in many places on this river for miles together; the other indians now surround the herd on the back and blanks and at a signal agreed on all shew themselves at the same time moving forward towards the buffaloe; the disguised indian or decoy has taken care to place himself sufficiently night the buffaloe to be noticed by them when they take to flight and runing before them they follow him in full speede to the precipice, the cattle behind driving those in front over and seeing them go do not look or hesitate about following. . . .

By 1836, travel to the Great Plains was fairly common, but before then, even the reports of such authorities as Captain Benjamin Bonneville were discounted. Bonneville described a herd of the shaggy beasts as darkening the whole horizon. He stated: "I climbed upon a high bluff that gave me a wide view of the surrounding plains. As far as the eye could reach the country seemed blackened by the enumerable herds of the Indian cattle or buffalo."

In early days, the herds ranged in practically every section of the country—from the Atlantic seaboard to the Rockies; from Mexico to the subarctic. Like the deer of different regions, they varied in size, color, and other characteristics. Biggest of all was the "woods buffalo" of the Canadian north, along the Mackenzie River and in Great Slave Lake Country. A somewhat smaller type roamed the western slopes of the Rockies; there were not many of them and they disappeared early. The East had its coal-black, humpless "Pennsylvania buffalo," which lived in the hardwood forests and grazed in the adjoining grasslands.

But the greatest, the biggest buffalo herd of them all was made up of the magnificent "plains buffalo." He ranged what scientists believe was the original buffalo country—the midwestern and western plains from the Mississippi to the Rockies. He was big, though not so big as the "woods" type. A typical full-grown plains bull—one about seven years old—stood

16

The buffalo was free to roam the length and breadth of the plains, from Texas to Canada.

five or six feet high at the shoulder and weighed seventeen to eighteen hundred pounds, which was about the average weight. There were bulls, however, that approached a ton or more in weight.

The average bull sported horns fourteen or fifteen inches long, but again, many had longer ones. The record-breaking horns taken on a trophy, a Wyoming bull, have an outside length of 22⅜ inches and maximum spread of 35⅝ inches.

From deep in Mexico to the Great Slave Lake in Canada, and from the Rocky Mountains to the Mississippi, lay the great pasture lands of the bison. Tens of thousands crossed the "Father of Waters" and roved the eastern forests and grassy valleys to the Atlantic Coast, but these were mere stragglers from the countless numbers who preferred the open and unprotected stretches of the western prairie.

This vast expanse of Great Plains that bordered prairies and foothills was alive from end to end with huge masses of the shaggy humpbacked cattle. Sometimes millions gathered in one herd; between 60 million and 75 million buffalo roamed over 3 million square miles of the rich grasslands. No lowing or bellowing arose from the limitless herds, only a muffled, far-off snorting sound. For the only sound a buffalo makes is a sort of snorting, such as we ourselves can make by expelling the breath sharply between loose lips. Only in an aggregate of angry animals can the sound rise to a roar. These gatherings were untended except for the ever-present shadowy gray wolves and coyotes who hung upon the fringes in a grim semblance to shepherding dogs.

One fact is inescapable in the buffalo's story—he and civilization could not get along together. There would have been little practical value in attempting to domesticate him, even if it could have been accomplished. Among other considerations, his meat was definitely inferior to that of the domestic steer. Permitted to run wild, he was far too destructive to remain a neighbor of the wheat farmer. Imagine what a herd of buffalo could do, and frequently did, to a farm or plantation! And there was one final fact: The buffalo occupied the very land the white man wanted and needed.

The eastern buffalo was the first to go, since the East was the first land to be fully cultivated. As farmers cleared away the forests, the black bison gradually fell back to the West before them. Finally, he was driven by hunger into raiding the farms. Retaliation was

19

A full-grown bull.

The Scavengers of the Plains," a drawing from the February 24, 1872 issue of HARPER'S WEEKLY.

The Four Great Buffalo Herds
The Great Plains 1870

0   50   100   200   250
Miles

swift and merciless. The settlers considered the bison as much of a nuisance as the gray wolf and hunted him accordingly. By 1800, there were only a few buffalo left east of the Mississippi, and by 1820, there were none at all. On the other side of the continent, Spanish settlers were busy exterminating the Rocky Mountain bison.

Even so, as late as 1867 the western herds were still so large they interfered with all forms of travel. The steamer *Stockade*, then in the charge of Captain Grant Marsh, was held up for over a day while a snorting, wallowing herd of buffalo crossed the upper Missouri River in front of the riverboat.

In the same year a Union Pacific train going from Omaha to Cheyenne was stopped twice by the shaggy beasts crossing the tracks in front of it. In 1869, the buffalo were thick as flies in western Kansas. A herd crossing in front of a Kansas Pacific engine held up the fast mail train for over two hours.

In 1871, Major Richard I. Dodge drove a buggy southwest along the Arkansas River toward Fort Larned, Kansas. He reported: "The whole country appeared one mass of buffalo, moving slowly northward. Only when among them could it be ascertained that the apparently solid mass was an agglomeration of enumerable small herds of fifty to two hundred animals. This great herd was about five days passing to a given point, and not less than fifty miles deep. From the top of Pawnee Rock I could see from six to ten miles in every direction. The whole space was covered with buffaloes, looking at a distance like one compact mass, the visual angle not permitting the ground to be seen."

No one really knows how many buffalo wandered on the plains of North America before the explorations of the early fifteen-hundreds. The most carefully calculated figures range between 70 million to 80 million head. Remember, this was during the primitive period of Indian hunting. As late as 1850—after gunpowder had begun to take its toll—over 50 million shaggies were still left out West.

All paintings of early buffalo hunts show a scene in which a man, Indian or "paleface," is mounted on a fiery, charging horse. He is riding his sturdy steed directly into the herd, downing the shaggies with a rifle, six-shooter, lance, or bow and arrow.

They did hunt like that in the early days, but it was not the typical method. The Indians found easier ways to kill the buffalo, with much less effort and personal danger.

During the eighteen-seventies the white hunter of hides slaughtered the buffalo from a "still hunt." He crawled toward the herd against the wind and lay behind a rock or bush, then stuck the heavy rifle on a Y-shaped stick. His long-ranged weapon brought down scores of the animals without alarming the rest of the herd.

The Indians, especially the Blackfoot of the northern prairie, often drove herds of buffalo over a cliff. The creatures were maimed or killed by the fall over the *pishkun*.

The American *Bison* or buffalo was the largest wild animal on the continent and could

he woods buffalo of the Canadian
orth was the biggest of the species.

be extremely dangerous when aroused. The size, appearance, and habits of the bison explain why they were often called Indian cattle. The shaggy-haired buffalo differs from a domestic cow mainly because he has a hump on his back and a larger head. There is a mat of hair over his front parts that protects the animal, as he always grazes into the wind, even in the dead of winter.

The drifting snow, numbing cold and wind of the blizzards that swept the plains created fear and dread of winter in men and beasts, except the buffalo. Whether the storm lasted but a few hours or many days, the animals turned their thickly furred heads and shoulders into the wind and waited patiently.

For this, they had grown the long woolly fur on their forequarters, often twenty inches in length. For this, they had forgotten unreasoning fear and learned to stand quietly, to conserve their strength to dig through the snow for food when the storm was over.

Nor was the penetrating wind a total evil, for it would blow enough snow from some areas to make their foraging easier. This calm acceptance of the storm, plus the bisons' instinctive knowledge of how to combat it, probably was the greatest single contributing factor to their survival on the plains in such great numbers.

In spring, the swelling tides of buffalo rolled across the land as inevitably as the seasons. While there were no long annual migrations, there was a general northward movement of the herds to follow the grass as the green of spring softened the dead brown and white of the winter. From horizon to horizon, the surface of the land flowed with the dark carpet of the foraging beasts.

The early tenderfoot thought the buffalo was stupid for the buffalo has very poor eyesight. But, the animals have an acute sense of smell, and can run like the wind. They were built for speed, despite their big heads and heavy haunches. Their run is a heavy gallop; many a horse could not win a race with a galloping buffalo bull.

The shaggies needed a huge amount of grass and water, which kept them constantly on the move. A herd would consume most of the grass on one range, then migrate slowly into the wind searching for fresh forage. Every three or four days, they would come down to water and drink their fill, usually at night.

24

The individual bison was anything but smooth coated. The time of the northerly trek

A group of bison gallop, single-file, down a dusty Montana tra

Crow warrior with buffalo shield.

was also the period for shedding the long winter coat of matted woolly fur, and was the most unbeautiful interval in the seasonal span of buffalo existence. He was a patched-up job of bare skin, loose, sunburned old fur, and darkly gleaming new pelt. In the spring, the monarch of the plains resembled a soiled old comforter in the final stages of coming apart.

But in the autumn he stood forth in all the shining glory of his sable-colored winter robe. He was magnificent. At this time he was probably the grandest and most impressive representative of all his species. The powerfully developed muscles of his neck and shoulders imparted to his sharp, dangerous horns a dynamic force so swift and effective against his enemies that his bearing was one of arrogant self-assurance. But, like all other animals whose species becomes numerous, the bison was also possessed of an inordinate sense of security in his great numbers. All the familiar hazards were well under control, and there was nothing new under the bison's sun—that is, before the appearance of the white man.

In normal years, with the grass grown thick and well over two feet high in the big pasture, the herds did not stray far from the section where they wintered. In dry years, with the grass shorter and more sparse, the herds spread out and traveled farther. Then the pasture land of the plains was a tinderbox. Fires, started by lightning or Indians, often blackened great areas of the prairie. When a herd came to one of these burned-over regions, the leaders plunged ahead without hesitation. An unerring sense directed them across the wasted space toward the nearest water and grass; it might be a day's march or one of many days' duration.

This constant grazing into the wind led the herds of buffalo only a hundred miles in each of the four directions. The annual migration was a moderate swing northward and southward, for the mass of buffalo drifted with the changing seasons and the changing prevailing winds.

The herd would move at a slow, leisurely pace and each animal would nibble at the grass as he went along. Frequently they would stop and ruminate, chewing their cud contentedly the same as does a domestic cow. However, any sudden fright could convert the slow, leisurely grazing of the herd into a deadly stampede. Sometimes the bark of a prairie dog or the rustle of a wind-blown leaf was enough. The approach of a grass fire would send the buffalo stampeding across the prairie for many, many miles.

In their blind rush, many a buffalo would become mired in the quicksand or in a

26

Some bulls weighed as much as a ton, and had horns of matching dimensions.

treacherous small stream, or the lead animals would plunge to death over a steep cliff. If the stampede were on the open plain, however, it would wear itself out in time and without any harm.

During the midsummer days, the blubbering snorting of the mating bulls could be heard for miles. This sound would carry even farther than the rumbling of a stampede. Travelers as far as three miles from a herd could hear the uproar of the excited bulls. When the herd was in stampede, the ground would shake for miles around from the thundering, tearing hooves.

As the swift, tiring journey of a stampede continued throughout day and night, the deadly patience of the wolves was rewarded, for the young calves, the cripples, and the aged were unable to keep up. The weary beasts that dropped behind the main herd were isolated and dragged down by the constant enemy, the gray wolf.

Swollen rivers also took their toll of the herds, but here the losses were usually among the very old animals, for the young calves, finding the current and width of the river too much for them, would climb astride the hump of the nearest swimming adult to be ferried

Indians hunting buffalo in midstream, depicted in the May 16, 1874 issue of HARPER'S WEEKLY.

over the remaining distance. The crossing of one of these rivers in flood might continue for several days, with a traveling herd of buffalo more than thirty miles wide and sixty miles long, a common sight before 1865.

With the arrival of summer and abundant grass, the animals fanned out over a vast area, dividing into numerous smaller herds that grazed along gradually. Indian hunters, disguised in the skins of wolves or young buffalo, moved cautiously about the fringes of the herds to procure food and skins for the tribe with their silent arrows.

Plagued only by wolves, Indian hunters, and the hard-biting flies, the buffalo's summers were spent in comparative peace and well-fed contentment. They dug great holes in wet spots on the plains, where they wallowed until coated with a thick layer of mud that dried into an effective coat of armor against the stinging flies. Many of these ancient "buffalo wallows" are still visible on the western plains.

Throughout the autumn, the movement of the herds was generally to the south, toward the region chosen for the winter grazing. There, they would await and weather the storms that came raging out of the north. When spring again broke the grip of winter, they would move out on the great circle as they had always done before.

Usually the leader of a herd of buffalo was an old cow; the bulls positioned themselves outside the main body as guards. During the winter, the bulls and cows grazed in separate groups while the calves followed their mothers.

In late spring the calves were dropped. At that time the bulls were more attentive: They stood on guard to keep the wolves away from the young who gaily played about. Frequently, a wolf who came too close would be tossed high into the air by a bull and be killed from the fall to the ground. An angry bull buffalo has been known to give mortal wounds even to raiding bears.

The buffalo cow was a careless mother and looked after her offspring in a lackadaisical fashion. She would desert her calf whenever danger approached. At times she would hide the calf in a brush pile; but the calves were slow to learn. It was estimated by the Plains Indians that the wolves killed a third of all the calves born every year.

It was during the calving season that the old hair fell out and a new coat was grown and the animal looked tattered and naked. It was a bad time for the buffalo; without an

Many a calf perished on the plains because of the indifference of its mother.

Two hunters disguised in wolfskins, as painted by George Catlin.

armor plate of mud and hair, they were at the mercy of swarms of mosquitoes and other stinging insects.

During this shedding period, the buffalo indulged in his favorite habit: wallowing in the dust. Buffalo wallows were the mudholes where the shaggy could roll and plaster himself with mud, but if there was no water just any dusty old pit would do. Both dust and mud gave protection against pestiferous tiny biting insects. A buffalo wallow was usually eight to fifteen feet across and two to three feet deep.

Such wallows or depressions saved the lives of many early plainsmen, for they often yielded a scout or traveler enough dirty water to quench his racking thirst. The buffalo wallow proved to be a handy refuge from Indians on the chase. From its shelter many a pioneer or hunter held off a band of Indian warriors until nightfall, when the attack would lift. The Plains Indian could not fight in the dark, for if killed in the night, his "spirit" could not find its heaven.

Upon the horizon of the bison's quiet prairie world there appeared a disturbing phenomenon, an ill omen. The three ships of Columbus flitted about for awhile and then were gone. Such fragile, evanescent little specks to play so fateful a part in the lives of nearly every living thing on the vast continent of North America!

Soon there were more ships, many more, along the shores far to the south of the pasture lands of the big plains—ships that brought men seeking gold, not buffalo.

When the stories of the seven gold cities brought the seekers northward, three new threats appeared under the bison's sun: white-skinned men, guns, and horses.

Of the three, the horse was destined to play his part first against the buffalo. The Spanish guarded their precious horses closely, but some escaped nevertheless into the southern section of the big pasture. There, under the beneficent influence of sun, tall grass, and absolute freedom, the horses multiplied rapidly into herds. Before long, the Plains Indians learned to ride.

Buffalo and Indian

It **is fitting** that the five-cent piece of yesterday had a buffalo on one side and an Indian head on the other. For the life and economy of the Plains Indian depended entirely on the buffalo.

The wise old woman of the tribe was said to have "buffalo wisdom." The white buffalo was believed to be the child of the sun god and was worshipped accordingly. The Indian spoke of "Our Father the Buffalo," the gift of the "Great Spirit."

All the tribes of the plains regarded the buffalo as a gift from their "Great Spirit." The shaggies were their private herd of cattle and not to be tampered with by the white intruders.

The Comanche on the southern plains depended on their best scouts to find herds for their tribe. Sometimes they asked the aid of a medicine man, who told the "legend of the buffalo" with appropriate rituals and ceremony. The story the Comanche shaman told was like the buffalo legends of all the Plains Indians:

> *The earth was made and so were the people [Indians], but there were no buffalo. One day, an old man came and watched the young men playing games. He stood with his quiver on his shoulder, then he put it on the ground and went into some nearby bushes to relieve himself. While he was gone, the people looked into his quiver and saw the good fat meat. Day after day, the stranger came back to watch the games and always the people looked into his quiver. It was always full of fine fat meat.*
>
> *They asked the owl to find out where he got this fine meat, and the owl flew over the mountain and perched at the old man's lodge. At the old man's lodge, the owl saw a stranger and his wife with their*

35

small daughter inside. They were eating of the fat meat. The owl flew back and told the people. They moved their village near to the old man's lodge on the other side of the mountain. The stranger saw them and became angry and threatened them. They waited, frightened, but wondering how they could get some of the meat.

Finally, a young medicine man said he would find out, and he changed himself into a young dog. Then, while the old man was away from the lodge, he crept up to the door, whining. The young daughter of the old man took pity on him and opened the door. The dog went in and saw a great hole in the ground. He looked through the hole and saw a wide plain covered by many, many buffalo.

The dog-medicine man thought of a very clever idea. He began to bark and shout into the hole until the buffalo became nervous and started to stampede. They ran up out of the hole in the earth and smashed down the old man's tepee. They covered the earth from sky to sky. That was how the people got the buffalo.

All of the Plains Indians agreed that the buffalo came from a hole in the earth, and the buffalo was from the inside of Mother Earth herself.

The buffalo was everything an Indian needed except firewater—and he could be traded for it. As long as the buffalo abounded, it was simply impossible to vanquish the nomadic Indian tribes. They could stave off the U. S. Army as long as they had their movable food supply. The buffalo made the Indians so independent, they could afford the arrogance of defying the "Great White Father," his impotent rage and attempts to bring them into his camps.

The Army man who is versed in the military history of the West will tell you that, only after the Army decided the buffalo must go and then put the dictum of free ammunition into practice, did it make any headway against the Plains Indians. The buffalo went fast— 7 million to 10 million decimated in a ten-year period. He was not popular with Congress. And our conquest of the Indian kept pace with the destruction of his herd of curly cows.

37

Plains Indian on horseback.

"Slaughtered for the Hide," from the December 12, 1874 issue of HARPER'S WEEKLY.

These full-sized wax figures i_ the Luxton Museum at Banf_ Canada, depict the Sun Dance _ the Blackfoot brave. Note th_ buffalo skull hanging from th_ skewers in his back.

Congress never passed a solemn resolution proclaiming that the buffalo be killed in large numbers. Nor did it issue a direct order that the men of the Army turn into buffalo hunters. The method was more subtle, but just as effective: Hide hunters were encouraged, even subsidized with free ammunition.

The medicine men of the many tribes used the buffalo's hides and skulls in their religious rituals and dances. The Blackfoot and Mandans of the Upper Missouri Valley practiced a great variety of buffalo rituals. The one ritual, however, that was common to most plains tribes was the Sun Dance.

The Sun Dance of the Blackfoot was the most cruel, the most dangerous of all. It was performed by first cutting the skin of the breasts of the young braves, inserting into the incision bone skewers, then attaching these skewers to a central pole by a rawhide rope.

Similar slits were cut into the backs of these young braves and bone skewers were inserted in these cuts. A decorated buffalo skull was then hung from these bone skewers. The purpose of the dance was to worship the sun and the "Great Spirit." It was a giving of thanks to the Creator of the buffalo.

The braves danced, without food or water, and blew on an eagle-bone whistle until their very exertion had torn free the bones holding them to the central pole. Scars and severe infection usually followed the Sun Dance. If the cuts were made too deep and the skewers imbedded into tough muscle, as many as three braves would be required to pull on the buffalo skull to tear loose the bones and finally free the dancer.

Besides the Sun Dance, special songs were chanted, and some tribes even had dreamers who went into a trance and saw visions. Their visions "told them" exactly where to go for the best buffalo hunt.

The Mandans prayed first to the Great Spirit and then addressed the deity of the herd: "Great bull of the prairie, be here with your cow." The Sioux, the Assiniboin, and the Pawnee engaged in elaborate ceremonial dances before and after any hunt.

The Comanche hunters used, in addition to their best scouts, a number of rituals to ensure their success.

Frequently, they would catch a horned toad and ask it where the buffalo were hiding.

40 Then they put the toad on the ground and watched in what direction it scampered. They

The Buffalo Dance of the Mandans, as drawn by Carl Bodmer in 1834

This George Catlin painting gruesomely portrays the Mandan torture ceremony, in which buffalo skulls dangle from the flesh of the young braves.

believed he would go in the direction of the nearest herd, the one the Great Spirit had selected for their hunt.

The Comanche's hunting dance was always performed before the men went out on a hunt, by the light of a campfire, or better yet, in the full of the autumn moon. Drummers, singers, and dancers would perform until midnight.

After a successful hunt, the entire tribe held a buffalo-tongue ritual and shared a great feast. The women roasted fresh buffalo tongue over an open fire, while the men seated themselves in a half-circle about the fire. At exactly noon, the medicine man would light a pipe and blow puffs of smoke toward the sun, the earth, and toward each of the four winds. This was a thanksgiving for the good fortune the Great Spirit had bestowed upon them.

The pipe was passed to each hunter, who in turn went through the same smoke-blowing ritual. Then, a woman of purity and virtue served the roast tongue to the successful hunters.

The buffalo drives of the Blackfoot of the northern plains were community or tribal enterprises, carried out by all the members of a band. A ritual that centered about the "buffalo stone" was performed before the start of a drive.

The "buffalo stone," a fossil marine shell bearing a close resemblance to a buffalo bull, was found in special areas on the northern plains. To the Blackfoot, it was a strong magical charm with great hidden powers that lured the buffalo to their death.

Legend states that the stone reveals itself only to a virgin woman, and instructs her in a certain number of songs. These songs would influence the buffalo herd so that the people of her tribe would be triumphant in their buffalo drive.

During the last part of the ritual a man and woman, usually husband and wife, teamed together to perform the necessary songs and imitative buffalo-mating dances. Frequently, they were helped by friends, a necessary part of the before-the-drive rites and ceremonies.

The songs and dances, which lasted most of the night and early into the morning, were to ensure the safety and success of the "runner" in his activities during the drive. The outcome of the drive was entirely dependent upon the good fortune and skill of this one lone man.

The runner was a young unmarried man who underwent extensive training that hardened his body, built up his endurance, and developed his running speed. With his disguise made from a buffalo robe and a head mask, he was a skillful decoy for the herd to follow

Buffalo meat laid upon a rack of wickerwork.

in all innocence during the length of the Indians' drive.

It was the runner's task to locate the herd and start it up in a mild stampede, then lead it toward the corral or a steep cliff. If there were plenty of buffalo, finding the herd was easy. If there were not, the runner might have to run many a long mile before finding a good herd.

The second part of the runner's task, to start the herd into a stampede, was a chore requiring the greatest skill and knowledge. The runner frequently made his way around the entire herd once or twice, then started up the leader. Once the leader was started, the entire herd followed blindly in panic.

The runner's success depended greatly on the darkness of the early morning and his disguise as a buffalo. The Blackfoot brave acting as a runner was scarcely distinguishable from the buffalo in the herd.

The runner or decoy trotted beside the lead animal and the balance of the herd followed, strung out behind. He regulated his speed and direction very carefully. To guide the shaggies into the openings of the drive lanes leading to the corral or cliff fall required perfect timing. The decoy led the herd on until the first light of dawn appeared in the east.

Back at camp, many preparations were under way. A scout waited on a hill, watching for the approach of the herd. With his first glimpse of the running animals, he ran back to the lodges with the news. Quickly, the hunters took their stations along the drive lanes. They hid behind the markers, one Indian brave behind each rock pile. Each hunter crouched on his knees, a buffalo robe held outstretched before him. The brave was concealed, not by the rock pile, but by the buffalo robe.

As the herd passed at full gallop, the hunter twitched his robe, confining the charging shaggies to the lanes leading to the corral or cliff. The runner kept even with the leader of the herd.

The runner continued leading the herd until he reached a shelter dug especially for him just a short distance from the cliff. As the animals passed each of the hunters along the drive lanes, the braves fell in behind the herd, shouting and whooping as loud as possible. The noise helped drive the buffalo forward.

As the shaggies drew nearer and nearer to the edge of the cliff, the danger increased. The Blackfoot braves were intent, anxious, nervous.

This 1905 postcard, a collector's item, depicts a young brave teaching his brother the glories of the buffalo hunt.

The moment of greatest danger was at hand. The lead animal must jump over the cliff, for if it had the strength to turn back, the entire herd would turn with it. The buffalo would reverse their course and stampede madly into the hunters, killing many Indian braves. If the lead buffalo plunged over the cliff, or *pishkun*, the entire herd would blindly follow.

This is how the Indians in Montana got their meat and hides before they had horses. There are more than thirty of these *pishkun* sites in Montana.

Because the *pishkun* was "prehistoric," there are many things we do not know about it. In general, however, it is known that the "rock lanes" were often placed to form a rough V-shape on the plain above a cliff or steep bluff. These lanes, which often extended back above the cliff for several miles, consisted of small piles of rocks spaced about fifteen or twenty feet apart. The lanes formed a sort of a funnel, with the narrow end at the very edge of the cliff. Such lanes may still be seen today at the *pishkun* sites.

The buffalo were maneuvered very painstakingly into the wide mouth of the funnel, then at the proper time they were stampeded toward the edge of the cliff.

There is little agreement among anthropologists as to how the buffalo were kept within the lane. Some authorities think that tall sticks were inserted in the rock piles, and that pieces of fluttering hides tied to the tops of these sticks kept the buffalo in the lanes. Others feel the braves held and twitched the robes. Perhaps the Indians crouched behind the rock piles beneath a robe or skin, and at the proper moment, rose up to flutter a skin at the now-panicked herd to keep them in the lanes.

These *pishkuns* usually were staged in November or December; in some cases, the same site was used again and again. The sites were, of course, located where the buffalo were accustomed to graze and where an appropriate drop existed. The drop-off varied in height from 30 to 150 feet. In some places, the drop-off was merely a steep bluff, and in others it was a sheer cliff. Today, the bases of such *pishkun* sites are rich grounds for anthropologists. Many thousands of arrows and spearheads have been taken from such excavated areas.

After the shaggy-haired buffalo herd made the jump over the cliff or was driven into a box canyon, the animals were killed with a bow and arrow or a large stone hammer.

The Blackfoot women and children, accompanied by their dogs, came running from the village and immediately a feast was held. Choice portions such as the tongue, the heart,

An artist's diorama of stamped-ing buffalo falling to their death from an Indian pishkun.

John Mix Stanley painted "The Buffalo Hunt" in 1842 while he was at Fort Gibson in Indian Territory.

and the liver were hurriedly cut from several of the animals, hauled back to camp, and cooked for the hunters to eat. If none of the hunters had been injured or killed, prayers of thanks were offered up to the Great Spirit.

Different hunting practices were carried out by different groups of Plains Indians; however, all Indian buffalo hunting was divided into three main types.

At first, the Indians drove the buffalo on foot. Later, the advent of the horse facilitated the drive. The third method is shown in the classic pictures of the Indians hunting buffalo: The Indian brave astride a fiery charger is seen attacking a surging mass of buffalo, riding in close, and killing them with bow and arrow or lance.

This running hunt was not effective until after the Indians acquired horses, and it involved a rather spectacular chase. The Indians of the plains watched with envy as the wild mustangs raced freely over the land where he, man, slunk with the coyote. So, first one horse was captured, then others were caught. Slowly at first, then as the possibilities became evident to the Indian, there was a concerted rush for horses. No longer was he forced to wait in hunger for the buffalo to come to him. He left his earth and brush dwellings, built buffalo-skin and pole lodges that could be transported easily, and followed the moving herds across the Great Plains.

This change in the Indians' mode of living was one of the swiftest and most complete of any ethnic group in the history of man. Astride his horse, the Indian's ancient feeling of kinship with the coyote changed quickly to an attitude of dignified lordship over the Great Plains. Almost overnight he became the master horseman. And the buffalo chase on horseback became the most colorful, exciting, and dangerous game in all America.

At this time approximately three hundred thousand Indians depended solely, or to a very great extent, upon the buffalo for their existence. They still believed the Great Spirit sent these animals forth in a steady stream from a great hole in the earth and that the supply would never diminish. Despite this faith that the buffalo would be forever plentiful, the Indian killed only what he needed and wasted nothing. His was a true buffalo culture. The huge beasts furnished him with clothing, bed, lodge, utensils, and most of the decorative ornaments that brightened his life. Therefore he used the precious gift sparingly.

The tongues were roasted or boiled fresh, or cured by first steeping in cold water, then

The Indian was quick to become the master horseman in the dangerous game of the buffalo chas

This George Catlin painting of an Indian hunting buffalo with a lance was published in 1844.

in tepid water. Finally salt was rubbed into them. The roasted marrow bones were the parts of the buffalo most relished by the traders and travelers.

Buffalo meat that was to be dried was cut into thin slices, wound about sticks slanted over a slow fire, or laid upon a rack of wickerwork. Sometimes the heat of the sun alone was enough for drying. To make pemmican, dried-out slices were pounded into a flaky mass. Then an equal weight of melted fat was poured over successive layers of these shreds. Buffalo fat was far more palatable stuff than the fat of domestic cattle and any quantity, plainsmen said, could be eaten without fear of indigestion. So, this layer loaf of alternate meat and fat, packed in bags made of buffalo skin, was a nutritious, compact food that remained acceptable to the taste indefinitely. Pemmican became the standard food of the fur traders.

Buffalo robes—the winter skin of the buffalo, when his coat of hair was at its thickest, blackest, and handsomest—were dressed by the Indian women. The fur traders never bought untanned robes; no white men could attain the exquisite workmanship of the Indians.

The method of dressing the robes varied among the various tribes. The Crow Indians were probably the most careful of all. No tribe could match in beauty the work of the Crow women. First, they immersed the buffalo hide in a mixture of ashes and water for a few days. This loosened the hair. Next, they pinned the skin taut to the ground with tapering stakes through the edges, scraped off the loose hair, and shampooed the skin with handfuls of the brains. The women then dried and thinned the skin by graining it with a sharpened bone, usually the shoulder blade of the buffalo. A final process of smoking the skins assured that they would remain soft and pliant whenever they got wet.

A white buffalo—so great a rarity that even the Great Spirit must have been surprised when the first was born—received its due reward of awe from most plains tribes. To the Mandans, especially, the skin of a white buffalo was fine, powerful medicine, and a good white skin would bring the price of ten or fifteen horses. Three or four years after the purchase, piety demanded that the skin be offered to the sun and wind and rain.

The Indians of the Plains trained their fleetest horses to run close beside the shaggy buffalo. Even after the Indians had guns, most of them preferred to shoot the buffalo with a bow and arrow. The bow was short so that it could be handled easily on horseback; the arrow was tipped with a piece of sharpened flint or iron. The skilled Indian hunter could shoot

A good part of the catch was dried and stored for the long winter months ahead.

Cree hunters drive buffalo toward the pound.

Indian buffalo pound, pictured in John Franklin's NARRATIVE OF A JOURNEY TO THE SHORES OF THE POLAR SEA IN THE YEARS 1819, 20, 21, AND 22.

arrows as fast as the white man could fire a Colt six-shooter.

Usually, the Indian brave tried to hit the buffalo behind the short ribs, with the arrow ranging forward into the lungs. If a hunter put too many shafts into an animal, the laughter of the squaws rang out loud and clear when they retrieved his arrows. The chase was not the best method for the Indians to get their winter supply of meat; the drive was by far the most efficient. But no matter by what method the Indian hunted the animals, he found use for each and every part of the buffalo.

The butchering was done by the women of the tribe. The hunters would leave a cow lying on her side, but the heavier bull was heaved over onto his belly. The squaws slashed across the brisket and the neck, then folded back the hide so they could cut out the fore-quarters. The joint was used to separate the bones. The women slit the hide down the middle of the back and peeled it down toward the ground. This made a clean area on which to place freshly butchered meat.

The hindquarters were disjointed and the rump was left attached to the backbone. The flank was cut open, the stomach and intestines removed. The liver and heart were considered choice morsels. Bits of intestine, cooked with its partly digested food, was a tempting and favorite dish for the Indian.

The squaws bagged the meat in the fresh hides, loaded it onto pack horses, and took it to the camp. Then the tedious work of slicing and drying most of the meat began. The hides were pegged out, hair-side down, to dry. The tongues were finally smoked over a fire of buffalo chips. These smoked tongues became a popular delicacy in the Eastern and European restaurants of the eighteen-fifties.

The meat was carefully smoked or dried for the winter, and again, a small fire of buffalo chips and green twigs was used to preserve it. The meat was cut into strips that followed each muscle bundle lengthwise and thus made a long thin strip.

Some meat was sun dried with the squaws "jerking" the flesh. They pulled it into longer and narrower strips as it dried in the hot prairie sun. The dried, pulled buffalo muscle was known as the "jerky" of the plains. It would keep forever and a day.

The Indians used various other methods of preserving the flesh. Pemmican was packed in bags of buffalo hide. It, too, would keep for years. Some of the Plains Indians flavored

The albino bison, sacred to the Mande

andan corpses were laid out in buffalo skins to decompose.
terwards, the skulls were arranged in a circle around two
ffalo skulls (George Catlin sketch).

Catlin drew these Sioux squaws working on the pegged-out hides.

Seneca buffalo mask,
worn by dancer in ritual.

their pemmican by mixing in various nuts and dried berries. When fresh meat was plentiful, pemmican was made and stored for the cold, long winters ahead. Yet, it was commonly eaten at any season of the year. Many of the white traders and visitors called it "Indian bread." Sliced and dipped in wild honey, it was a tasty and nourishing dish.

On the southern plains, the pegged-out buffalo hides were dampened with water for ten days. This water contained mashed buffalo brains. The skins were rubbed and kneaded once a day to make them soft and pliable before smoking. It was a laborious process to scrape the flesh from the hides with a flint blade, then work them into a soft robe. Robes were not smoked as were ordinary hides, but were decorated with colored figures. These soft robes were used for coats and bedding. Some were cut and made into caps, mittens, and leggings. The smoke-tanned hides were used for tepee walls, moccasins, saddle bags, and shields.

Sometimes the hides used to cover a tepee were first soaked in water until the hair fell out. Then they were tanned with brain water and smoked. It would take as many as twenty hides to make a single tepee; the average was usually sixteen.

Some tribes sewed the raw or green hides together and fitted them over wooden frames to make bull-boats. Narrow strips of rawhide were plaited, to make lariats and tie ropes. The strong leaders from the neck and back provided stout thread for sewing.

Bowstrings and snowshoe webs were made from the tendons; the hair was woven into ornaments and twisted to make ropes. The buffalo's bladder became a container for marrow, or was converted into a canteen for carrying drinking water. The bones were used for spears and tools of all kinds. A shoulder blade served as a hoe, smaller bones as scrapers. Up North, a toboggan was made from the backbone, covered with a bit of rawhide. The horns provided drinking cups and spoons. The back fat was used as hair grease, and the gall as yellow paint.

The buffalo chips were just as valuable to the Indians as the meat and hide. Throughout the Great Plains, wood was scarce; buffalo chips served as a standard fuel. They remained dry inside even after a soaking rain and always burned slowly with a hot, clean fire. It was more of a glow than a flame, but perfect for camp cooking.

Years before the railroad penetrated into the great herds, and before tanners in England and Philadelphia learned how to make serviceable leather from the buffalo hides, the thick-furred buffalo robes tanned by the Indian women gave warmth to several generations of

Americans. A fine squaw-tanned robe was worth several times the price of a hairless skin.

Then, across the plains, there formed a trickle of white men. The trickle grew to a stream. Boats appeared on the rivers. Forts were built at strategic spots, and dwellings sprang up around them. White-topped wagon trains rattled into the big pasture. The white men built houses and fences, and plowed the buffalo's grass under. There was a growing unrest among the Indians. It bred scattered raids upon the whites by the more warlike tribes.

Then, a hunting party came across a scene that kindled a slow anger in the plainsman's breast: the telltale tracks of oxen and wagons and the white man's iron-shod horses, and nearby, the carcasses of many buffalo. Some had not even been touched. From others, only the round, black tongue and the tastiest part of the hump had been removed. Of them all, only one had been skinned.

The scene reappeared, again and again, in other parts of the Great Plains. The smoldering coals of anger were fanned to the fire of rage. This waste of the Indians' staff of life, the gift of the Great Spirit, was incomprehensible to him. Council fires burned through the long nights over the great central region of the big prairie. What kind of beings were these vile wasters? The people of the plains knew they could not share their land in peace with such men as these.

The flames of war swept across the plains like wildfire. The many tribes were united in only one thing: hatred of the white man. Each tribe tried to protect its own grounds from the spoiling of plow and gun. But bows and arrows were poor weapons against rifles and, one by one, the tribes were defeated or pushed further westward. The Indian watched in grim desperation as the stream of white men became a flood. He had to have guns, or he would be lost!

The white traders wanted Indian-tanned buffalo robes, since their own tanners never learned to equal the Indians in this art. The Indians had observed how the traders seldom allowed a thing like loyalty to their race to interfere with an opportunity to turn a quick profit. So, with these white men, he exchanged his buffalo robes for guns with which to kill other white men. Cap and ball, and old flintlocks, discarded by the whites as almost useless since the invention of the breechloader, were still guns to the Indians. Most of them would still shoot.

63

Obtaining the guns was a slow process. The Indians never acquired enough to go around. With traders demanding an ever-increasing number of robes for a gun, the Indians were forced into the ironical position of killing the buffalo in an effort to save him, and themselves.

In the early days of the fur trade and mountain men, the buffalo robe was a staple article for trade. In January, 1675, Marquette noted the Illinois Indians were willing to trade three buffalo robes for a cube of tobacco. The French Canadian traders and Hudson's Bay Company entered into this profitable trade in 1770. After Lewis and Clark opened the Northwest in 1806, Americans soon became interested in trading for buffalo robes. John Jacob Astor traded for both buffalo robes and beaver fur with equal skill. His company flourished from 1807 to 1843. True, he was more interested in the beaver pelt than the buffalo robe. But, after 1830 the buffalo robe replaced the beaver as the main item in Indian trade.

Buffalo robes were bought with trade goods rather than with money. These early fur traders took every advantage. Whiskey was one of the best trade items. A pint of watered-down rot-gut was traded for a buffalo robe worth at least five dollars.

Robes were traded for blankets, tobacco, axes, beads, hand mirrors, food, and other small items. A trader could obtain a fine buffalo robe for a bead necklace that had cost him only sixteen cents. On the upper reaches of the Missouri River, a trader could buy a robe for three cups of coffee and six cups of sugar.

Pierre Chouteau, a St. Louis trader, ordered six thousand pairs of French blankets, three hundred guns, three hundred dozen butcher knives, and nine thousand pounds of blue and white chalk beads, five hundred pounds of pigeon-egg beads, and a quantity of calico from one English firm. These were his trade goods for barter with the Plains Indians of the Upper Missouri River.

In 1803, only 850 robes were shipped east; by 1815, twenty-six thousand were shipped down the river. The average trader got a robe for $1.50 and sold it for four dollars. Some of the robes were sent downriver to New Orleans, others were sent east to Pittsburgh. In 1828, New Orleans received 199,870 buffalo robes.

The last big year for buffalo robes was 1844; 54,450 were shipped into New Orleans. Trade in robes was still brisk in 1857; the American Fur Company shipped seventy-five

thousand to the East. By then, buffalo were scarce in some parts of the Upper Missouri River Valley. In the fall of 1858, William T. Hamilton had a most profitable year trading with the Blackfoot and Crows in Montana for robes and smoked buffalo tongues.

Hamlin Russell said in 1874, "One could buy a beautiful fur robe overcoat, well-made and lined with flannel at the retail clothing stores in St. Paul for $10.00." By 1875, the trade in buffalo robes had completely ended.

Meanwhile, the white men went into the buffalo-hide business. By 1860, millions of buffalo were killed for their hides alone. But it was slow work transporting the hides to the riverboats by wagon and the hide hunters clamored for cheaper transportation. In 1865, the Union Pacific Railway built west from Omaha into the heart of the buffalo's range, and made the marketing of untanned hides very profitable for the white man.

As the railroad advanced, the bison herds retreated to the north and south of its path, since the hide hunters had killed all the animals found near the line. Using the railroad as a base of operations, the hunters outfitted expeditions and followed the retreating animals. This action split the universal herd and divided the American bison into what became known as the northern and southern herds.

The relentless destruction of the buffalo was bitterly opposed by all the Plains Indians. This led to many serious problems, and many Indian uprisings and Sioux "ghost" dances marked the tension. It was their grave concern over their supply of meat, this destruction of their "cattle," that motivated the Indian attacks of the sixties and early seventies on the Great Plains.

The relentless killing-off of the Plains Indian's cattle would force him onto the reservations, even more effectively than would all the efforts of the United States Army.

The Dudes Come West

Even before the Civil War, the eastern sportsman found the shaggy buffalo a tempting target. He, and his European counterpart, came west to see if the stories they had heard were true. They went out to hunt buffalo for pleasure and sport, beyond the fringe of the frontier.

The Indians rarely hunted for pleasure alone; they killed the shaggies when they needed meat or hides. Major Richard I. Dodge remarked, "The Indian is a great epicure, he knows the choicest tidbits of every animal and how to cook them to his taste. The great Fall hunt yields him the fullest enjoyment of his appetite. The warrior who kills buffalo will cut it open and eat at once the raw liver."

One of the first easterners to go west for the excitement of the chase was Washington Irving. In the fall of 1832, he toured the Southwest with Henry L. Ellsworth. Count de Pourtales from Switzerland and his tutor, Charles J. Latrobe, were also in the party. The group traveled by steamer from Cincinnati to St. Louis, then overland to Independence, Kansas, and Fort Gibson—Indian Territory.

On October 10, 1832, a fine fall day in the Indian Territory, the party set out on horseback with Pierre Beatte as their guide. The travelers swung down into the central part of the Territory, where they were pleased to find a large herd of buffalo.

They spent several days chasing the shaggies. Washington Irving was impressed and wrote, "There is a mixture of the awful and the comic in the look of these huge animals . . . They heave their great bulk forward with an up-and-down motion of the unwieldy head and shoulders. Their tails cock up like the cup of Pantaloon in pantomime, in the end whisking about in a fierce yet whimsical style; and their eyes glare venomously with an expression of fright and fury."

On October 29, Washington Irving killed his first buffalo. He had poor luck at first;

67

he was inexperienced and used a pistol to shoot at his prey. When he borrowed a double-barreled gun from Latrobe, his luck changed. He brought down his first buffalo the very same day. The guide, Beatte, removed the tongue and gave it to Irving, who proudly carried it back to camp.

Many hunting parties followed. In 1843, William Sublette, a fur trader, led a hunting party out onto the plains from St. Louis. The Scottish nobleman, Captain Sir William Drummond Stewart, and friends were in the party. William Clark Kennerly, a nephew of William Clark (of Lewis and Clark fame), wrote a detailed account of this trip.

The party, he reported, set out in great style. Wagons were loaded with provisions of flour, sugar, hams, tinned meats, pickles, brandy, whiskey, and fancy wines. Stewart, the Scotchman, drew gales of laughter from the frontiersmen of early St. Louis; his white jacket and straw hat seemed completely out of place.

When they later saw that he was an expert horseman and crack shot, they took an entirely different view. The party went into the broad valley of the Platte River and "encountered buffaloes in numbers which gladdened the heart of Sir William, who had come four thousand miles to shoot them."

The horses and men dashed along beside the shaggy monsters. Then the hunters would reach over, put the muzzles of their guns on the buffalo's shoulders, and fire. The eighty men left the prairie strewn for miles with the bodies of the dead shaggies.

Many, many buffalo were killed by the group, far more than were needed to supply fresh meat for the party. What sportsman could resist the temptation of the surging, tumbling mass of buffalo, spoiling to be hunted down? They took about eighty pounds of meat from a one-ton animal. Only the back strip, hump, and the tongue were used as food by the party.

Kennerly, Clark's nephew, reported a herd estimated to contain over a million buffalo. He wrote: "The pounding of their hoofs on the hard ground, sounded like the roar of a mighty ocean, surging over the land and sweeping everything before it."

The hunting party thus found more game than they had bargained for. But they had placed themselves in a tight squeeze, between the herd and the bank of the Platte River. They were directly in the herd's path and in grave danger of being trampled to death by the angry bison.

Much sport was made of the dude on a buffalo hunt in the O
West. "Turn About Is Fair Play," by Currier and Ives, 187

The greatest of all the mountain men, Jim Bridger, was known far and wide as "Old Gabe."

They contrived to turn the leaders off into a different direction. For two days the party labored, with guards of shouting men during the day and huge bonfires at night. Finally the danger passed and they were able to return safely to St. Louis.

Twelve years later, an even larger and more expensive hunt took place. In the spring of 1854, a wealthy Irishman spent half a million dollars on a buffalo hunt: Sir St. George Gore left from St. Louis and covered six thousand miles during the next three years. He was accompanied by forty servants and several scientific companions. During the entire hunt they lived in great luxury, with three milk cows, twenty-one two-horse carts, four six-mule wagons, two three-yoke ox wagons in the train, and one wagon alone filled with firearms of all types.

Gore slept every night in a brass bed, inside a fancy carpeted tent of striped green linen. He drank only the finest of imported wines with his meals. With a pack of forty greyhounds and staghounds to chase the game on the prairies, the party hunted beyond Fort Leavenworth and pushed deep into the wilds of the Northwest.

It was during the winter of 1854-55, which Sr. St. George Gore spent at Fort Laramie, that he met "Old Gabe," the most rugged of all mountain men, a tall, buckskinned fellow whose real name was Jim Bridger. Gore engaged Bridger as a guide and, after the spring thaw of 1855, the party headed up the North Platte and into the Powder River country. With Old Jim Bridger leading the way, they drifted down the valley of the Powder to the Yellowstone, and up the Yellowstone to the mountains.

The country was full of buffalo and other game, a hunters' paradise. The party rested during the winter of 1856, and in the spring, went hunting along the Rosebud and into the Black Hills. They broke up late in the spring of 1857. It was said they had killed 2,000 buffalo, 1,600 deer and elk, 105 bears, and endless numbers of prairie hens and other wild fowls.

Gore's expedition caused great resentment among the Indians of the northern plains. They complained to the officials in Washington, but it did them little good.

Finally, the Government intervened on behalf of the Wyoming Indians, whose food supply was being destroyed before their very eyes: Gore went back to Ireland. But it did nothing else to prevent the extermination of the bison. In fact, when other important foreign personages indicated a desire to hunt in the West, the Government often assigned high-ranking Army officers and detachments of cavalry to assist them.

The competent professional hunters—men who had a considerable investment in equipment—despised the amateur invaders. And for good reason: They wanted to keep the buffalo-skin business for themselves, rather than see it ruined by men who killed five buffalo for every skin they managed to sell. The professional usually shot only as many bulls as their skinners could handle. Why waste effort and ammunition—especially when factory-loaded cartridges sold for twenty-five cents apiece on the plains? The seasoned skin hunters were frugal; most of them reloaded their own cartridges and were not likely to waste them. Some even cast their own lead bullets.

Fancy hunting parties of European nobility were not the only ones who hunted the buffalo. Soldiers from the frontier outposts went on drunken shooting parties. The farmers and pioneer merchants from the fringe settlements went out on many a buffalo hunt. The meat was brought back and helped fill in their meager food supply. When the buffalo were plentiful, only the hump and tongue were eaten. The rest of the huge animal was left for the wolves.

Herds of buffalo retreated from the roadway of the Union Pacific, leaving a strip fifty miles or more barren of any wildlife. When, in 1867, Major Powell traveled the Union Pacific to its terminus, then near Cheyenne, he saw only one live buffalo, an old bull wandering aimlessly along the bank of the Platte.

The same year the golden spike was driven that completed the laying of the trans-Pacific railway the Kansas Pacific was building across Kansas to Denver, the Atchison, Topeka, and Santa Fe was throwing its rails across the wagon ruts of the Santa Fe Trail. The southern herd was hacked by the advancing lines of travel that, for seekers of profit or pleasure, opened the way into the heart of the buffalo country.

In the autumn of 1868, this new field for pleasure seekers really opened up. The buffalo, associated with everything wild and daring, could now be hunted indolently, under the comforting auspices of business-eager railroads. Excursions at very low rates were announced—from Cincinnati, Chicago, St. Louis. Railway stations bore placards that read:

73

ny early settlers fed their families in lean times by collecting buffalo bones and selling
m. Shown here, a settler's typical dugout with its sod roof and part-log construction.

EXCURSION

An Excursion train will leave Leavenworth, at 8 A.M. and Lawrence at 10 A.M. for

SHERIDAN

on Tuesday, October 27, 1868, and return on Friday. This train will stop at the principal stations both going and coming. Ample time will be had for a grand Buffalo hunt.

Buffaloes are so numerous along the road that they are shot from the cars nearly every day. On our last excursion our party killed twenty buffaloes in a hunt of six hours.

All passengers can have refreshments on the cars at reasonable prices.

Tickets of Round Trip
from Leavenworth
$10.00

Refreshments were served on excursion trains for shooting buffalo. An original drawing from LESLIE'S ILLUSTRATED, *June, 1871.*

Sheridan, a town near the Kansas-Colorado border named for General Philip Sheridan, was then the "end of the tracks" for the Kansas Pacific. But building was going on beyond and a town was being surveyed for the next terminus—this to be complementarily named for Kit Carson.

Sheridan remained the terminus for a year and a half, and developed into the most flagrant of hell-roaring railroad towns. Gamblers, horse thieves, murderers, and gaudy ladies aplenty were present among its population of two thousand—with its Metropolitan Bars, Imperial Hotels, and Palace Ballrooms. Occasionally, whiffs of gunsmoke could be discerned among the other unsavory odors of these public buildings. Eventually, a Committee of Safety was formed and warnings were posted for various ladies and gentlemen to leave town within forty-eight hours. The honor of being the terminus carried with it a substantial freighting trade, with bull trains and mules that carried merchandise to Colorado and New Mexico and returned with ores and buffalo hides.

The Union Pacific hired hunters to kill about twenty-five buffalo. The choice portions were brought to camp by pack mule and wagon, where the cooks prepared the fresh meat for the hungry workers.

Down in Kansas, a young man with a .50 Springfield breech-loading rifle called "Lucretia Borgia" was hunting for the Kansas Pacific Railroad. A few years later, this twenty-one-year-old would be known as the famous "Buffalo Bill."

William F. Cody was born in a log cabin on an Iowa farm in 1846. He went to Kansas with his father when he was eight years old, and at eleven, worked as a mounted messenger and a horse herder. A short time later, he rode briefly for the Pony Express.

Young Will's mother died in 1863, and in February of 1864, he enlisted in the Union Army. In 1866, at twenty, he married and tried running a hotel. He turned to freighting, but on his first trip the Indians captured his wagons and horses. Our future hero even tried land speculations in Nebraska along the Union Pacific right-of-way.

For sport and a few choice morsels of meat, Will rode out and shot buffalo. He was skillful at this exciting pastime. Mounted on his horse, Brigham, he would chase a large buffalo across the prairie, the horse and rider neck and neck with the buffalo. One shot from Cody's big gun, and down went another buffalo.

William "Buffalo Bill" Cody at twenty-two.

The Nebraska land bubble burst and Cody went broke. He tried his hand at grading road-bed for the railroad, but the blisters on his hands were not to his liking. The Goddard Brothers contracted to feed the railroad construction crew, and they wanted a hunter to bring in fresh buffalo meat, so at twenty-one, Will Cody became a professional buffalo hunter.

Will was a good shot and killed plenty of meat for the railroad camp. He learned to approach a small herd of buffalo on foot, and to shoot as many as he could in a single "stand." This did not have the thrill of the chase, but was effective and sure in supplying fresh meat.

The railroad built farther west, but Will Cody stayed in Hays City, Kansas, to hunt buffalo and to sell the meat in town. He would kill and sell as many as nineteen buffalo in three days. During the next few years, Cody was a scout for the military under General Eugene A. Carr.

Will Cody was an average young man on the frontier, perhaps a better shot than most, a talent that did little to bring him fame. His luck would change in the late summer of 1869.

At age twenty-three and out of a job, he was loafing in Nebraska near Fort McPherson. A visitor from New York, a man by the name of E. Z. C. Judson, was there also. Judson, an

author of dime novels, wrote and edited under the pen name of Ned Buntline. Judson, or Buntline, saw William F. Cody as the type of frontier hero he had been seeking for his adventure stories.

He coined the name "Buffalo Bill" and attributed to Cody many deeds that had actually been performed by others. When these did not satisfy him, he concoted from his active imagination other even more daring deeds, always startling and dramatic.

Bill liked the publicity, grew a goatee, long hair, and wore fringed buckskins. He looked the part of the frontier hero, and cashed in on his newly-found reputation. It was not long before Buffalo Bill was sought after as the favorite guide of the eastern sportsman. When the Grand Duke Alexis of Russia wanted to go on a buffalo hunt, naturally he hired Buffalo Bill.

This was the most publicized buffalo hunt of all times. The son of the Czar of Russia was backed by the United States Government and General Philip Sheridan. The general arranged for the hunting party in 1872. The Grand Duke went by train in his fancy private car to the Kansas frontier town of Hays City. Sheridan arranged for Chief Spotted Tail of the Sioux to stage a war dance for the royal visitor. Buffalo Bill taught the prince how to shoot and allowed him to ride his new and favorite mount, Buckskin Joe.

The young prince forgot the advice Bill had given him and completely missed the first buffalo. He picked out another, and managed to put a couple of pistol shots into the animal. The wounded shaggy charged down a ravine, but Cody arranged for the Grand Duke to kill the panting bull. The Grand Duke dismounted and slashed off the tail as a trophy, then sitting on the dead buffalo, he shouted and yelled in Russian. The other hunters rode up to congratulate and toast the young prince with champagne.

The publicity that Will Cody received from this hunt and his other exploits soon made him a hero on the vaudeville stage and in the circus.

Visitors from everywhere were hunting buffalo. Travelers on the Kansas Pacific always took potshots from the open windows of the passenger cars. They left the shaggy victims, wounded and dying, for the wolves and buzzards. Many of the noble beasts were slaughtered by excited passengers on the early western trains.

79

The Buffalo Hunt," by Currier and Ives, 1872, is believed to represent Buffalo Bill on the right and his hunting protégé, the Grand Duke Alexis.

"The Great Royal Buffalo Hunt," by Louis Maurer;
Buffalo Bill is in the foreground, Grand Duke Alexis to
his left.

East of Sheridan, trains might flank herds of bison spreading far over the plains. The buffalo had not yet learned to take flight at the sight of the steam engines. If buffalo were traveling in a course across the railway, away they went, charging across the ridge on which the iron rails lay, determined to head off the locomotive and cross in front of it. It often happened that buffalo and cars ran side by side for a mile or two, so near that the passengers could almost clutch the buffalo by their manes. The car windows were opened, and breechloaders flung hundreds of wanton bullets into the animals.

The daily train was a "mixed" affair with freight cars carrying quartermasters' stores or goods for the railroad commissary, and sometimes, stock cars bringing remounts for cavalrymen, followed by one or two passenger cars. It left Lawrence for the West at ten in the morning, and at a speed of fifteen to twenty miles an hour, continued through the flat monotonous plains. During the day the train passed Fort Riley, an old Army post, stranded in a district where there were no longer any savages. The post was reduced in dignity to a stockade for antiquated cavalry horses.

Farther west, the train passed Abilene—a hotel, a few shanties, and a number of cars upon a side track—the small town that in time would fatten on cattle droves brought across unfenced ranges up the Chisholm Trail from Texas.

As dusk came on, a single straggling buffalo or a small herd of antelope might be seen from the train. It was now at the fringe of the buffalo country.

At eight in the evening, the train arrived at Ellsworth. Farther west, there might be Indian war parties; and because of this, in the autumn of 1868 the Kansas Pacific ran beyond Ellsworth only in daylight. The passengers accordingly were "booked for the night." Ellsworth boasted a hotel, the Anderson House, which could accommodate some of the passengers. Others were billeted on the citizenry, or sprawled out in the cars. Rudolph Keim, going westward to join Phil Sheridan, the commandant-general of the department, enjoyed Room Number One of the Anderson House, but he left a doubtful endorsement of the hotel:

> *After a supper on buffalo steak, antelope ham, soggy bread, and a cup*
> *of warm water, flavored with a grain of coffee or a leaf of tea, the*
> *passengers gathered in the hotel office, a small room eight by ten fur-*

nished with a counter and several dilapidated chairs. The proprietor presided. Seating himself on a three-legged chair and cocking his feet on the stove.

The gentleman entertained his guests with yarns laudatory of his own career, and bits of the red-rich history of Ellsworth in the days when it was the railroad terminus. Since the railroad had pushed farther west, the town had become quite orderly. Keim complains of "violent yells" and "salvos of uproarious oaths" throughout the night, but there was no actual shooting.

At daybreak the train was ready to depart. This event was announced just in time to allow a last round of drinks, as "with a parting benediction upon the landlord's head most of the passengers retired to an adjacent rum mill and stowed away a slug or two of mountain dew to keep up their spirits."

The locomotive whistled "up brakes" and snorted out of Ellsworth. The luxuriant prairie grass gave way to the stubby, deep-rooted buffalo grass. An occasional woodpile or water tank, watched by a squad of soldiers with a dilapidated freight car for their sleeping quarters, was the only railway station along to the west.

As the morning brightened, Rudolph Keim could see spots along the horizon—small herds of buffalo. In the car in which he was seated were twenty-five stands of arms, breech-loading rifles, and a chest of needle cartridges provided by the Kansas Pacific for its employees. Each passenger carried his own weapons.

Suddenly, shots rang out from the forward car; the trainmen rushed to the rifle rack and armed themselves. Keim wrote:

At this juncture as I thought things were getting serious I re-examined my own rifle, buckled on a pair of pistols, slung my cartridge-box over my shoulder and started forward to look into the cause of the commotion. At this moment a shout "Buffalo crossing the track!" was heard and bang! bang! bang! simultaneously went several pieces. Poking my head out of the window I observed a small herd of six buffalo bulls

85

The railroad passengers' pastime.

running at full speed parallel with the train, and about a hundred yards ahead and not more than sixty feet from the track. They seemed bent upon crossing, but finding the locomotive pursuing too closely, they swerved away. Instantly the engineer slackened the speed of the train, to accommodate the fusiliers. The barrage wounded two of the buffalo; the locomotive whistled down brakes, and without waiting for the train to stop every one, passengers, engineer, conductor, brakeman, jumped off the cars and gave chase.

One of the wounded buffalo was still on his feet. Keim described the animal's predicament:

> . . . and with great effort was trying to escape. He had been shot in the thigh and though retarded made good progress, when another ball taking effect in the other leg, let his hind quarters down upon the ground. Nothing daunted the wounded animal made every exertion to drag himself off, on his two fore feet, when a ball under his shoulder put an end to his suffering and his efforts to rejoin his companions. A cheer wound up the railroad chase, when the busy knives of "professionals" in hip-joint operations, soon had the "rumps" severed and after cutting out the tongues and a few strips of "hump" the rest of the two immense carcasses was left as a dainty and abundant repast for the wolf. The meat was put on the train, and again we continued our journey.

About noon the train reached Hays City, only a shell of a railroad town; all the restless spirits moved on to Phil Sheridan station, a hundred miles away to the west.

The train carried few passengers past Hays City—these fierce, hirsute, and unwashed. Now large herds of buffalo could be seen; and thirty miles from Hays City, the prairie was black with the curly cows. The conductor buckled his pistol belt about his waist and kept his rifle near him.

A number of small herds that crossed to the south upon the approach of the train invariably raised their heads, looked for an instant, and then with heads down and tails up, galloped across ahead of the locomotive. In trying this strategic feat, one specimen found himself forcibly lifted into the air and thrown into the ditch, where he lay upon his back, his cloven feet flourishing madly.

Several animals were shot out of this herd. The train now stopped to afford time to bring in a few rumps. While this operation was going on, a party of six or eight started down the track to dispatch the buffalo, still kicking and bellowing with a mixture of suspense and

87

Left for the wolves after losing his hide.

rage. When the party got within fifty yards, a shot was fired that seemed to have a vitalizing effect. With one desperate bound the old beast regained his feet. Several more shots were instantly fired, but none seemed to take any effect. Instead of retreating, the irate bull made for the party, coming at a full jump with head down, tongue out, bleeding and frothing at the mouth, eyes flashing—and to cap the climax of his terrible exhibition of fury—roaring fearfully. As there was no time to lose, and to fire at him "head on" would be a waste of ammunition, the party scattered in all directions. Losing sight of the hunters, the enraged animal, smarting from the blow received from the locomotive and the tickling he sustained from the rifles, vented his anger on the other side of the embankment of the railroad by digging great furrows in the earth.

Three of the party fired, and instantly, the animal fell to his knees.

For sixty miles the same great multitudes of buffalo carpeted the earth. As the train approached Sheridan, the herd thinned out to isolated bulls, then even they disappeared. At six in the evening the train drew up at tracks' end, marked by a wooden milepost that announced "405 to S.L." The heart of the buffalo country was cut through and through.

By 1870, it seemed that the survivors of the smaller herds had joined the single great herd; and when this herd crossed the tracks in front of the locomotives, trains waited for hours. Engineers tried running through the buffalo, but when their engines were thrown from the track, they learned to give a closely massed herd the right-of-way.

Twice in one week, trains of the Santa Fe were thrust from the tracks by buffalo. An army officer remembered an occasion in 1871 when "the train entered a large herd, which scattered and seemed to go wild at the shrieking of the whistle and the ringing of the bell. As we went on the thicker they became, until the very earth appeared to be a rolling mass of humps as far as we could see."

Passengers to Denver and Salt Lake, on the Smoky Hill route of the Union Pacific, were offered frequent opportunities to shoot at buffalo from the windows and platforms of the cars.

The shooting of buffalo for sport continued into the eighteen-seventies, and in 1871 General Sheridan took a dozen of his Eastern friends on a hunting trip across the plains. James Bennett II, the publisher of the New York *Herald*, went along and reported on the trip.

The outfit had sixteen wagons, two of which were used just to haul ice and wine.

An enraged bull bison rises to the attack after a tumble in the dust.

Horse-drawn ambulances carried the hunters when they were tired of riding horseback. Again, the guide was young Buffalo Bill Cody.

The name "Buffalo Bill" was no longer reserved for William Cody alone. William Mathewson, who owned a ranch on Cow Creek, traded among the Comanche and other tribes for robes. He built a large trading post in Indian Territory, and was one of the first residents of Wichita, Kansas. During the summer of 1860, when severe drought and millions of grasshoppers left the pioneer Kansas farmers near starvation, Mathewson took some friends and went out buffalo hunting. He sent back a whole wagon train of meat to feed the hungry Kansas settlers. After that they called him "Buffalo Bill" in gratitude for his good deed.

Nicknames were common on the frontier; one of the hunters around Hays City went by "California Bill." In the fall of 1867 he brought many large loads of meat to town. Buffalo meat became a drug on the Hays City market, and the going price for prime hump dropped to seven cents a pound. Soon, great quantities of fresh buffalo meat were shipped by fast, iced express to St. Louis, where it was passed off as beef.

In the early fall of 1870, a hardy New England tough stepped off the train at Hays City, Kansas, who would prove to be more effective than anyone else in clearing the plains of buffalo. Blue-eyed and blond-haired, Josiah Wright Mooar was just nineteen years old. Immediately, he got a job chopping firewood, but on Sundays, he went out and killed a buffalo or two, which kept the wood camp supplied with fresh meat.

For five months Mooar chopped wood, but he did not come west for that kind of slave labor. He got together an outfit of three wagons and four men, and went into the more lucrative profession of buffalo hunting. The market for buffalo meat was still growing. The Easterners had developed their taste for the tongues and hams, which were shipped fresh during the winter. In summer the tongues and hams were iced or salted and smoked. The market was mainly for fresh meat. Hides were good only for making lap robes.

During the winter of 1870-71, hides were thrown away or left attached to the hind quarter, when shipped back east. The rest of the animal was left to rot on the prairie pasture.

Mooar and other hunters sold their fresh meat at Hays City. The price fell from seven or eight cents a pound to three cents, and buffalo steak was a common item on the menus of the poorest restaurants. Tanned buffalo leather had only a limited use, being too

. the thicker they became, until the very earth appeared to be a rolling mass of humps . . ."

soft and spongy for most purposes. Mainly it was good for belting and book covers. Unless the Eastern tanneries could find a way to make buffalo leather more useful, the hides would continue to be wasted and the market for meat glutted.

There was just no market for the raw, dried, or "flint" buffalo hide. One year would change this!

Slaughtered for His Hide

J. Wright Mooar, the mightiest of the hide men, was hunting buffalo near Hays City, Kansas, mainly for meat. While on the range he often crossed the paths of other hunters and soon became well acquainted with them. He knew Charlie Rath, A. C. Myers, and rugged Jim White.

Mooar teamed up with White and they hunted together during the winter of 1870-71. Mooar later recalled, "We would kill a buffalo, and cut it in two, right down the middle. We would leave the hide and hair on. We shipped the hind quarters and the saddles. The rest of each buffalo carcass, including the hide, we left to rot on the prairie."

Mooar and the others were killing the shaggies for meat. But, meat prices were steadily falling. Many a time, Mooar and Jim White would sit around the campfire in the evening, talking about the waste of the hides. If the hides could be made into useful leather, hunting the buffalo would be more profitable. One could hunt all year long.

In the winter of 1871, Charlie Rath told Mooar that W. C. Lobenstein had received an order for five hundred buffalo hides. The Leavenworth, Kansas, firm contracted with a tannery in England that wanted to experiment in tanning the raw buffalo hide.

Shortly before this, J. N. DuBois, a Kansas City dealer, had shipped several bales of the shaggies' hides to Germany. In the spring of 1871, DuBois sent out circulars offering to buy all hides taken.

His pamphlet told the hunters how to peg out the hides, flesh-side up for drying. He sold a special arsenic poison to kill the bugs infesting and damaging the untanned green skins. Mooar filled his share of the Lobenstein order and found he still owned fifty-seven hides. He shipped these to his brother, John, in New York City and hoped John Mooar could interest the American tanners in trying them.

One tanning company in Pennsylvania offered to buy them at $3.50 each. John readily

·ds of the plain, their reign soon to end.

accepted their offer, and a few weeks later, he was pleased to hear the outcome of the tests. The hides could be made into good leather, and they wanted him to send them two thousand more hides. He notified his brother, Wright Mooar, in Kansas, and within a short time, there were orders for all the buffalo hides they could possibly deliver.

John Mooar quit his New York job and went into the buffalo-hunting business along with his brother. The Mooars killed and skinned buffalo along the upper Arkansas River during the summer of 1872. Buffalo were plentiful and the two brothers shipped hides east all summer long. By this time Mooar had traded his Springfield rifle for one made especially for buffalo hunters, the new .50 caliber Sharps, with a range of about one thousand yards. The weapon, the Indians said, "shoots today and kills tomorrow."

Old Frank Mayer, hale and hearty and full of enthralling memories and conversation at the age of ninety-seven, hunted buffalo for a living longer than any other man—ten full years. He did not, for a good part of that time, have to invest his money in powder or lead. Uncle Sam gave it to him outright. The method of getting a supply of ammunition was delightfully simple, and completely bereft of the usual Army red tape.

"I would ride into one of the Army camps on a Sunday morning and seek audience with the commanding officer," he was quoted as saying. "We would sit and smoke. After awhile he would ask me if I could use some ammunition. Sure I could. Whereupon as much as I could carry away was all mine.

"I was young and callow in those days and thought it was my good looks or winning personality which was making the Army so generous with me." One morning, he mentioned this generosity to a high-ranking plains officer.

"What am I supposed to do with this ammunition—kill Indians?"

"Hell, no, that's our job," replied the officer. "You just kill buffalo. We'll take care of the Indians."

The officer explained the Army philosophy behind this largesse. "Mayer, either the buffalo or the Indian must go. There isn't any other way. Only when the Indian becomes absolutely dependent upon us for his every need, will we be able to handle him. Every buffalo you kill now will save a white man's life. Go to it."

This was all the encouragement Mayer and the several thousand other tough young

The Mooar brothers, Wright and John, went out after buffalo with outfits like this.

adventurers on the western plains needed. They went to it with a vengeance.

But the word spread nevertheless how easily a man could make his fortune killing buffalo. "There are millions of them," one Easterner would tell another. "They're easy to kill, and their robes sell for a hundred dollars. What are we waiting for?"

A horde of raggle-taggle adventurers began to pour westward. They were the newly discharged Civil War soldiers, carrying military muskets; ruined southerners seeking a new start in life; boys from the farms; clerks from the cities; ne'er-do-wells from everywhere. They carried a weird variety of guns—old cap-and-ball pistols, smooth-bore muskets, Kentucky rifles, and big Colt revolvers. They were to learn, however, that they could not make a fortune killing buffalo. In fact, most of them could not earn enough to even feed themselves. Buffalo hunting really was a job for the experts. But as fast as they quit, new recruits came to take

95

IMPROVEMENT IN RIFLES.

This is an improvement in Rifles, combining Sharp's Patent Loading Breech, and Dr. Maynard's Patent Self-Priming Rifles. In No. 25 of our last volume we published an illustrated description of Sharp's Rifle, and we would refer our readers to that for an explanation of the manner by which this rifle is loaded at the breech.

The accompanying engraving only illustrates the improved mode of priming, which is the invention of Dr. Maynard, of Washington. The engraving is a side view, with the priming box open; no caps are used; the priming is a patent preparation of percussion paper made into a coiled ribbon, represented by D, and placed in the inside of a small box, which is now represented as being open. F shows the edge of the lid; A is the hammer; E is the nipple of the priming orifice. It will be observed that the strip of priming ribbon passes over the top of the nipple. It will also be noticed that there is a notch in the end of

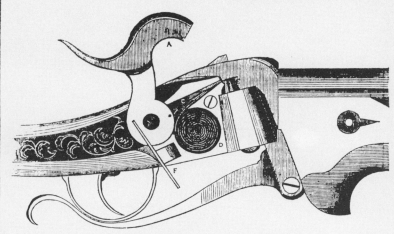

the hammer, A ; this cuts off the strip of ribbon as the hammer is coming down on the nipple, and when the hammer strikes the prepared paper, it being percussive, the powder is ignited, and the gun discharged. The question may now be asked, " how is the paper fed over the nipple for a new priming, after having been cut off by the hammer ?" This is done by a small flat steel spring, B, secured on the periphery of the ring of the hammer joint. When the hammer is drawn back, it will be observed that the flat spring, B, is moved forward, pushing the priming strip over the orifice of the nipple for the next discharge. When the hammer, A, falls down on the nipple, it will be observed, the spring, B, is drawn back for a new feed of the paper. This would draw back some of the paper, were it not for another small stationary flat spring, C, which holds the paper so as to allow it to be fed only up and along the metal incline to cover the nipple. This is the most ingenious, simple, and effective method of priming firearms ever discovered. Albert S. Nippes & Co. have the exclusive right to apply Dr. Maynard's Primer to Sharp's Rifle, with the exception of the U. S. Government privilege to the same. These rifles, thus improved, are manufactured and sold by Butterfield & Nippes, Kensington, Philadelphia. Capt. Tansil, of the U. S. Marine Corps, and a board of Ordnance officers, have reported in favor of the warlike instrument. A ball was fired by it along the surface of the Potomac, and it was loaded and fired again so quick that the two balls were seen skipping along the surface of the water at one time, a good evidence of the speed whereby it can be loaded.

their places. At the height of the massive buffalo slaughter it is very likely that from ten to twenty thousand hunters were in the field on the central western plains.

Although different hunters had different ideas of rifles, toward the tail-end of the buffalo days, the greatest and most deadly American rifle ever made came from Christian Sharps' Bridgeport factory. It was called the "Sharps Buffalo." Its caliber was .45-120-550. That means the cartridge was 45/100 of an inch in diameter, was loaded with 120 grains of black powder, and used a slug weighing 550 grains. It was a tremendous killer and would drop dead in his tracks the heaviest buffalo who ever sniffed and ate grass. It weighed 19 pounds, so a man did not sprint very fast while carrying it. But for its time and place it was perfect. Only about 2,000 of these rifles were ever made.

The bullets used in the big single-shot rifles of the day were not usually lubricated with wax or grease. They were "patched" or wrapped with fine linen paper. The patch was cut so that the two ends were at an angle and were just long enough to go twice around the bullet without any overlap. Putting on a patch required a certain skill, for it had to be smooth and even without any wrinkles. The end at the butt of the bullet was neatly twisted and tucked into a slight hollow at the base. The patch was intended to leave the bullet at the muzzle when it had served its purpose—preventing the sharp corners of the rifling from nicking the bullet and picking up lead.

Rifles using paper-patched bullets were the most accurate of their day. But, like all breech-loading black powder rifles, they produced their finest accuracy only when they were cleaned every few shots. The fouling of black powder builds up, caking in front of the chamber. This fouling deforms the bullets and cuts the paper patches. Target shooters using paper-patched bullets cleaned their rifles after each shot; the buffalo hunters could not do this. Their remedy was to pour water down the barrel. Often, lacking water, they urinated down the barrel. A stick rest for the long barrel was absolutely needed for hunting buffalo because of the weight of the rifle.

The story of those buffalo days is one of the great sagas of America, yet, I doubt if any other subject so close to home is so much misunderstood. Mention buffalo hunting to almost anyone, even a student of western Americana, and he will conjure up a mental picture of a man riding alongside the shaggy beast and firing his rifle or revolver directly into the huge body. Fire is snorting from the horse's nostrils, and everybody is having one hell of a good time.

It was one method of buffalo hunting, this running method. But it was merely a show-off's way—a stunt you reserved for when eastern folks were out West and you wanted to relieve the monotony by way of some fancy theatricals. Only amateur exhibitionists with horseflesh to spare used it. The professionals had a much more prosaic system, which made up for its lack of drama by being five hundred times more effective. It was known as "hunting from a stand."

Some smart hunter on the buffalo range had discovered an interesting quirk in buffalo psychology, a discovery that was to doom the entire buffalo herd. The buffalo normally was an animal that ran in small groups numbering ten to twenty individuals, most of the time. These groups were in the charge, not of a bellowing, mean old bull, but of a wise old cow. If a hunter isolated one of these little groups and shot the old lady herself, through the lungs so as to make her bleed freely, the others would not take flight or stampede. They would just stupidly hang around, nosing, sniffing the blood as it flowed pink from her nostrils, and would continue to mill around like politicians outside the polls on Election Day. You could shoot

down every last member of the herd and not start any fuss. This was called "making a stand"— the secret of successful buffalo hunting for hides.

The buffalo's disposition did not help him preserve himself for posterity either. At times he seemed the most stupid wild animal that ever crowded into the ark, with his poor eyesight, hearing, and sense of smell. He was not aggressive, all those pictures of a buffalo turning on his persecutors to the contrary. A good runner, his only instinct was to run. But then, the innocent calf did not think of running when his mother was shot through the lungs. So he was just plain doomed.

Most hide hunters used a forked stick for a rest and fired from the prone or sitting position. With a rest, the new Sharps was ideal for killing buffalo and the hide hunter soon developed the "still hunt."

A buffalo hunter went out before dawn. When he decided there was enough light to do his job, he would spot his first victim—always a cow. He would lung-shoot her; she would not drop. As he expected, she just staggered around while the other buffalo frantically smelled her and milled about. Firing as quickly as he could, the hunter would down the whole bunch.

It was about as exciting as shooting a dairy herd in the barnyard. The real hunting occurred when the hide hunter cautiously approached the herd against the wind, coming as close as possible without being seen by the nearsighted animals. He tied his horse to a bush and crept even closer. From a slight rise overlooking the herd, the hunter would take careful aim and shoot the old-cow leader. He fired round after round into such a stand. With each shot another animal would drop, for without a leader no headlong stampede from the scene of death occurred.

Billy Dixon killed an average of fifty buffalo a day in this manner, just exactly the number his skinners could handle. When finished with one bunch, he would turn to the next, probably not over fifty yards away from the first. Paying absolutely no attention to the excitement behind him, Dixon would repeat the process. Then he would turn to the third group, the fourth, and so on and on until he downed the number of buffalo his skinners could handle.

A good man who was careful enough so that the buffalo did not take fright could kill all the animals he needed, usually from a single stand, and quit work early. Mayer's largest

inishing off a wounded buffalo, as depicted in 1890.

J.H. MOSER.
WASHINGTON — D.C. 1888—

An 1874 drawing of the bison family.

"The Still Hunt," by James Henry
Moser, which hangs in the Smithsonian
Institution.

kill from one stand was fifty-nine; but Billy Dixon chalked up 101 without moving out of his tracks.

However, this did not establish any lasting record. Zack Light, a Kansas hunter, downed 74 shaggies with his Sharps Big .50 in a single stand. He killed 2,300 buffalo during one season. Wright Mooar shot 96 from a single firing position, and Kirk Jordan killed 100 in his best stand. In 1873, Charlie Rath shot down 107 in one morning on the Canadian River. Up north in Montana, Vick Smith shot over 5 000 buffalo during one season. Doc Zahl killed the record of 120 buffalo in one stand.

Tom Nixon, it is said, killed 110 head in forty minutes on the head waters of Bluff Creek in western Kansas. He used two Sharps rifles during this stand. When one became overheated, he opened the breech-lock and ran a wet cloth through, then he used the other gun until it was too hot to hold. Nixon was credited with killing 2,173 buffalo between September 15 and October 20 in 1875.

Wright Mooar estimated he killed over 20,000 buffalo in nine years of hunting. Doc Carver, the Nebraska dentist who later starred in Buffalo Bill's Wild West Show, claimed he killed 30,000 buffalo during his hunting career. Brick Bond is supposed to have downed 300 shaggies in a single day, and from mid-October to mid-December in the year 1876, took credit for 5,855 animals, an average of about 100 per day. Bond, who used a Sharps Big .50 with an octagonal barrel, was permanently deafened from the sound of his own gun. During his 1876 hunt, he kept five skinners busy.

The method of professional hunters such as these was a model of efficiency. The hunter, or runner, as he preferred to call himself—even though he did not even walk after his quarry, but lay hidden behind some hill from which to shoot—would scout for herds the day before. Once he had spotted his quarry, he would return to camp to clean his rifles, load his cartridges, and loaf.

The skinners worked hard and were smeared with blood, grime, and crawling insects early in the day. They were paid thirty to fifty dollars a month, though a few worked on a piece rate of twenty-five cents a hide. Usually they worked in pairs.

The job of skinning was always turned over to these menials, for no rifleman could ever stand the feel of a skinning knife in his hands; it contaminated him. When the hides were

Billy Dixon on the left and William Tilghman on the right, as they appeared in their buffalo-hunting days. Note the long barreled rifles they hold.

removed, the hide wagon would drive up, the hides loaded, and the outfit would head back to camp. The carcasses were left to the wolves. Once in camp, the hides were pegged out, roughly fleshed, allowed to dry. Then they were baled ten to a bale, and taken to Dodge City, Abilene, or Denver where buyers were waiting with the long green to pay for them.

The speed of the skinners was amazing. They propped the carcass in position with a "pritchell" stick. This was three feet long with one end sharpened and a nail driven into the other end. The nail was stuck into the carcass and the sharp end of the stick pushed into the ground. The dead buffalo was thus positioned on his back, with his legs thrown up out of the way. A pointed ripping knife, razor-sharp, was used to slit the hide from beneath the lower jaw, down the neck and belly to the tail. The hide was ripped inside each leg and a crescent-shaped cut was made around the neck, including the ears, but leaving the skin on top of the head. The hide was freed-up a little, and a rope tied around the neck flap.

A mule or horse was attached to the rope and the hide was peeled off the carcass. In most cases, they did not even take out the tongue or cut any meat. It was the hide, and the hide alone, the hunters were after. The skinners carried butcher steels in their belts to keep their knives razor-sharp and at every camp there stood a small grindstone. The green hides, which weighed eighty to a hundred pounds, were rolled up and thrown on a wagon. They were then spread out in camp on the grass, with the hair-side down, to dry and cure in the sun.

Arsenic, known to the skinner as "South American Bug Poison," was sprinkled on both sides of each green hide. This killed the maggots and buffalo flies that infested the hides and ruined them for sale. The hide was pegged down and held taut by driving sharpened pegs, six or eight inches long, through slits along the edges. A large bull hide might have two dozen pegs holding it down while drying in the sun. After three or four days of sunshine had dried the hides stiff as a board, the skinners turned them over and dried the hair side.

The hide, which was worth $2.25 to $3.50, is what lured many a boy away from a snug home to the hard, dirty, uninspiring career on the buffalo ranges. There were millions of these

Skinning a buffalo in 1874, on the Evans Creek Buffalo Gap in Texas.

"Doc" A. W. Carver, the Nebraska dentist who claimed he killed 30,000 buffalo. He later joined Buffalo Bill's Wild West Show.

105

curly animals running loose, many a young man figured, his for the shooting, each worth about three bucks. Suppose he killed only a hundred a day—three hundred dollars for a day's work. That was $2,100 a week—over $100,000 a year. A little figuring of this kind out around the livery stable, and the next day, a couple of adventure-struck kids would be high-tailing it for the Kansas or Nebraska buffalo ranges.

But, buffalo hunting for profit was not everything the book said it was. Mayer, for instance, a rather successful buffalo hunter in his ten years on the plains, when asked how he spent his tremendous profits, only smiled and dug into some old journals of his buffalo days. These revealed: His best year was 1878, when he grossed $5,435. Of this, $3,020 came from the sale of hides, $1,304 from the sale of meat, $905 from the sale of tongues, and $205 from fine specimen heads. That was his gross. By the time he had deducted expenses, he had left

just $3,124. And 1878 was his best year. His average earnings for the ten-year period was $100 per month.

Mayer figured the greatest profit was in selling first-rate hides. Some men skinned buffalo by cutting through the hide at the neck, putting a hook in it, and dragging it off with a horse. This method not only stretched the hide out of shape when it did not tear it, but sometimes left a good deal of flesh attached to the inside. When such a hide was staked out to dry, the flesh often went sour and spoiled the hide. Mayer demanded his skinners do all their work by hand. This was a real chore, since even rolling over a 1,500-pound carcass was work. In consequence, he got premium prices of from $3.00 to $3.50 for the hide of a fine buffalo cow. Bull hides, being too heavy for most purposes, brought only $2.00.

The finest hides, called "silks," were rare. Mayer claimed he got only 17 of these in all his hunting. A silk, as the name suggests, was a hide with an exceptionally fine, soft hair. They brought from $30.00 to $40.00 each.

In addition to hides, buffalo heads for mounting sold from $10.00 to $20.00 apiece and salted buffalo tongues sold for 50¢ each. Except for the tongues, buffalo meat was mostly wasted; though, occasionally a contractor with the job of providing meat for the men building a railroad was near enough to buy some. Even then, only the loin, hindquarters, hump, and tongue were purchased.

Many hunters began their hunts in Texas, working north as the buffalo traveled north following the grass as it turned green. They paused at those rivers that mostly run eastward from the Rockies across the Texas Panhandle and Kansas and Nebraska—the Canadian, Arkansas, Cimarron, Smoky Hill, Solomon, Republican, Platte, and their various forks.

Dodge City in 1872, the wagons loaded with buffalo hides.

Another view of the camp shows fresh hides stretched out to dry.

When the hides were fully dried, they were folded down the middle with the hair inside and piled in stacks. Most freighters could haul five hundred of these flint hides at a time. A sun-dried hide lost about half its weight and weighed about thirty pounds for a cow and forty pounds for a bull hide.

Most hunters hauled their own hides into town and sold directly to the hide buyer. A few buyers came out with their wagons to make the rounds of the larger hide camps. At first the wagons were drawn by oxen, but later on they were hauled by mules for more speed. No matter how the hides were hauled, they soon reached a railroad siding and were stacked in huge rows, awaiting shipment to the East.

Two new railroads, the Atchison Topeka & Santa Fe and the Kansas Pacific, built west across Kansas through the best of the southern buffalo range. Now, as William T. Hornaday relates, ". . . the rush to the range was only surpassed by the rush to the gold mines of California in earlier years. The railroad builders, teamsters, fortune-seekers, professional hunters, trappers, guides, and every one else out of a job, turned to hunt buffalo."

Many parties were still formed to hunt the animals for sport. A fairly typical entry in the

110

A common scene in 1874. In Dodge City, Kansas, stacks of buffalo hides await shipment east on the Santa Fe Railroad.

diaries of these sportsmen read: "Today we had the fine sport of killing sixty-three buffalo. We took some of the hump meat from one of the animals for our supper, leaving the rest to the very numerous wolves."

Everyone wanted the fun of killing, few wanted the labor of skinning. Uncounted thousands of animals rotted on the plains. During this period, the waste and loss reached such proportions that·each and every hide on the market represented five animals killed. Everything seemed to conspire against the few remaining herds. The new railroads gave easy access to the bison's favorite range, and there was great demand for buffalo robes on the market. Then, for the final touch, the flood of hunters brought with them the new Sharps rifle. Too many, and too fast, new things were appearing under the bison's sun.

If anyone got rich in the buffalo trade—and plenty did—it was the men who ran the big fur-trading houses. These fur traders handled a prodigious number of skins. One St. Louis, Missouri, firm shipped 250,000 hides to the East in a single year. In Fort Worth, Texas,

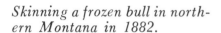

Skinning a frozen bull in northern Montana in 1882.

112

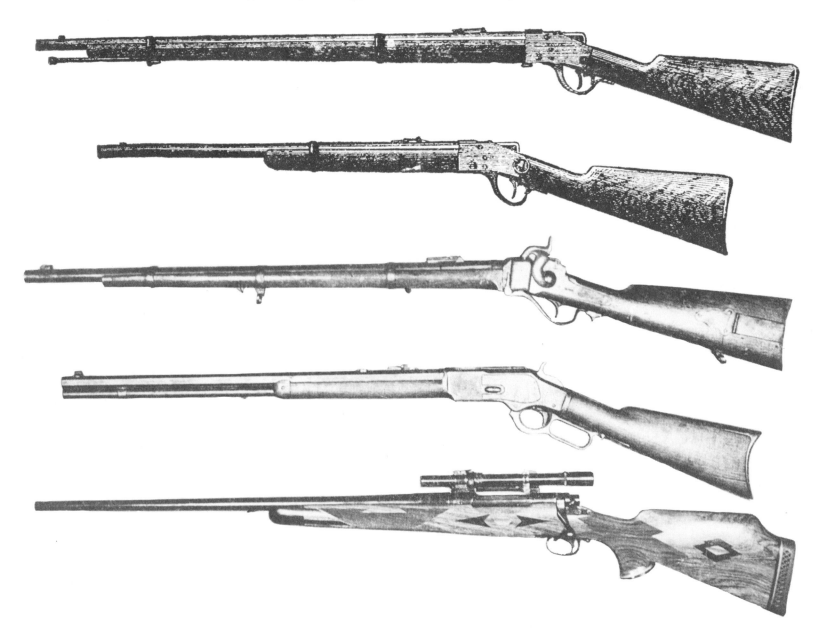

Contrast the Sharps rifles (first three from the top) and the Winchester 1873 (fourth from top) with the modern rifle at the bottom.

200,000 were sold in a one-day auction. A Dodge City, Kansas, company shipped 200,000 the first year the railroad reached town; other local firms freighted hundreds of tons of hides that same year, plus 200 cars of hind quarters and several cars of tongues.

When the Army began to open new posts throughout the West, it created a new market for fresh meat. The railroads, too, bought vast quantities for their construction crews. The renowned Buffalo Bill Cody is reputed to have killed 4,280 bulls during 1868 and 1869.

Most of the meat was wasted, for the laborers would eat only choice cuts of hump and tongue.

In the first three months after it reached Dodge City, the Santa Fe Railroad hauled 43,000 buffalo hides back east. The Wichita, Kansas, station shipped thousands upon thousands of hides, and as many as five freight carloads went out each day. A really small town, Great Bend, Kansas, shipped 4,850 hides in August of 1873. Major Dodge wrote: "I have counted a hundred and twelve carcasses of buffalo inside a semicircle of two hundred yards radius."

A few buffalo were left. West of Dodge City in 1873, a Santa Fe Railway construction train was held up for three hours while a herd crossed the tracks. When the Union Pacific reached Cheyenne in 1867, its east-west lines divided the plains buffalo into two mammoth herds—the "northern" and the "southern." Big as it was, the southern herd was doomed for early extinction; the Santa Fe reached the heart of its summer range in 1871, thus providing greatly increased shipping facilities. The train crews started carrying rifles. So did the passengers. Hundreds of animals would be killed and left to rot; other hundreds would be grievously wounded. The hunters worked feverishly; between 1871 and 1875 they killed $2\frac{1}{2}$ million buffalo a year in the Kansas Territory alone.

The hunters were doing their best to completely clear off the Kansas ranges. At one place on the prairie, a surveying party found sixty-five hundred buffalo carcasses. The hides were stripped and the untouched meat was left to rot. When the wind was from the west, the stink of this rotting mess drifted into Dodge City.

J. N. Helton, a Santa Fe Railway conductor, said, "I could have walked for a hundred miles along the right-of-way without ever stepping off a dead buffalo carcass."

The slaughter of 1872 and 1873 was great; the railroads hauled 1,250,000 hides out of Kansas alone. This so thinned out the Kansas herds that further hunting for hides was unprofitable. And, so it went until the buffalo runners one day discovered they were men without a job. They had been so thorough in cleaning out the shaggies on all the ranges that there were not enough of the critters left to fill a hide wagon.

It was only after all the hunting was ended that the runners discovered there never was a buffalo on the American continent. The animals they killed with so much aplomb were not buffalo at all. They were bison!

herd of grazing buffalo,
peace for the moment.

Showdown in the Texas Panhandle

Wright Mooar and a partner, John Webb, saddled their horses and took a trip scouting down into the Texas Panhandle. For five days they rode through a sea of grazing buffalo—an immense herd. Their report on the number of animals south across the Arkansas excited the other hunters.

The Treaty of 1867, however, had reserved these hunting grounds for the Indians. But Texas owned the land, and the state was not a party to the treaty. This gave Mooar an idea. He asked Major Dodge for advice.

Dodge replied, "Boys, if I were huntin' buffalo I would go where the buffalo are."

The hunters were willing to risk their scalps at the hands of the Indians, so they quickly formed parties and set out toward the Panhandle. The stubble-faced hide hunters knew the danger from the bands of Comanche and Kiowa who often slipped away from the reservation. The Indians rode the old trails to Texas to hunt buffalo, steal horses, and burn the cabins of settlers. They loved to scalp and take captives, and these Comanche and Kiowa resented the hide hunters more than did any of the other tribes of Plains Indians.

They killed whites at any opportunity; the high plains of the Texas and Oklahoma Panhandle were not safe for lone hunters. When the Mooars finally left Dodge City, there were two hunters and ten men for skinning and hauling in the party.

John and Wright Mooar crossed the Arkansas and drove south to the Cimarron. They went on through No Man's Land into the high flat plains of Texas and hunted in the brakes of the South Canadian River. This was the home of the Comancheros. These half-Mexican, half-Apache traders who came from the Mexican border towns were a rough bunch of men. They engaged in contraband trade with the Indians—guns and firewater for stolen horses.

One group of Comancheros attacked the Mooar camp four different times. The long range and accuracy of the Big .50 Sharps proved its worth. The Comancheros were beaten off each time without any damage or injuries to the Mooars. Despite the problems with the Comancheros and a fight with a band of Indians, the Mooar outfit found good hunting and took many quality hides.

The business depression and panic of September, 1873, ran the price of hides down. Dodge City dealers who usually paid $3.00 began checking each hide carefully for size and quality. In the winter they offered only $1.00 for a prime bull hide and $1.60 for a cow. Even with these prices, a hide hunter who was an expert marksman could manage to get along.

The Texas Panhandle was closer to Dodge City than to any railroad town in Texas. Hides were shipped back by wagon, and Dodge continued to be the "Queen of the Hide Towns." When Dodge City was first laid out, it was called Buffalo City. Kansas already had Buffalo and Buffalo Station, and Buffalo City proved to be just too much for the Postmaster General. He insisted the frontier village be renamed. It was then called Dodge City after Fort Dodge, five miles east of the Arkansas River. Dodge was well situated as an outfitting point and hide market, in the heart of the buffalo country, and the Santa Fe Railroad reached the new boom town in 1872. Money from the sale of hides burned holes in the pockets of the hunters and skinners and they spent it easy.

Dodge City quickly became "Hell on the Plains." It was full of whiskey peddlers, gamblers, and sporting women. Visitors called it the wickedest town in America. The best-patronized place of business was the saloon, and George Hoover and Jack McDonald opened the first. It was a wagon driven into a hole in the ground with the side let down to make a ramp leading up to the bar. Three other whiskey emporiums sprang up quickly. The most popular bartender in town was Dog Kelley, for he kept a pack of fancy hunting hounds. The saloons were open most of the night and a back room was set aside for gambling. The games ranged from five-cent chuck-a-luck to a thousand-dollar poker game.

On the south side of town, across the railroad tracks, were the sporting houses. This was a tough neighborhood and not safe for even a mean hide hunter. The Santa Fe station was a boxcar, but along the railroad siding, hides were stacked for nearly a mile. There were many crude buildings in town. The primitive two-story Cox House, with unheated bedrooms separated from each other by paper walls, was the best hotel. In the dining room, one could get a meal of pork and beans with hot pepper sauce, bread, and black coffee for seventy-five cents.

Zimmerman's Hardware Store sold any gun a hunter might want. It carried ammunition, harnesses, grindstones, knives, and all the other necessities. Patent medicines were available at the McCary and Fringer Drug Stores, while Rath's & Wright's and Myers' were well stocked with clothing and tinned provisions.

The Mooar brothers liked to sell their hides to LeCompte, who usually stood out in the middle of Front Street. Ready cash to pay for all hides offered bulged from his overcoat pockets, thousands of dollars in greenbacks. He kept each denomination in a separate roll, in a separate pocket of his great coat.

With the price of hides down and the scarcity of live buffalo along the Arkansas River, the hide hunters around Dodge City listened closely to Mooar and Webb, who brought back a fine load of hides from Texas. In the spring of 1874, forty hunters headed south with Charlie Myers. Myers had formerly been a hunter, but was now a successful merchant in Dodge City. He wanted to move his business to a better location. He loaded two wagons

118

Plains warriors, fast as the wind.

From the archives of the Kansas Historical Society, an actual photo of Dodge City's notorious Front Street.

of his own and all the empty wagons of the hunting outfit with a $50,000 stock of goods. He planned to open a new store in the Texas Panhandle. Each man in the party owned a saddle horse and was well armed and ready.

They were ready for Indians, as well as for buffalo. Among them were veterans of the Civil War and others more youthful and adventurous. Billy Dixon, Bat Masterson, Pat Garrett (later to be the celebrated killer of Billy the Kid), Dirty Face Jones, and James Hanrahan were all in the group. Hanrahan took along his hunting outfit with seven skinners and a stock of hard liquor. The firewater was for trading purposes, for he planned to open a saloon wherever Myers built his store.

The wagon train moved southward across No Man's Land, then on down to the main fork of the North Canadian, then on south to the north side of the South Canadian River. It was there, near the ruins of an old trading post, they decided to look no further.

Adobe Fort or Adobe Walls was built by William Bent in 1843, but his trading company abandoned it after a short time. In 1864, Colonel Kit Carson used the crumbling mud walls to win a battle against the wild Comanche. The buffalo hunters arrived at Adobe Walls nearly a decade after this battle. The remnants stood five feet high, but they preferred to build on a site a mile northeast.

There, Charlie Myers built a crude picket store, thirty by sixty feet, with a sod roof. Jim Hanrahan put up a sod house for a saloon, and between the two buildings, Tom O'Keefe built a picket blacksmith shop. All the buildings faced to the east, with no openings on the west. It was still called Adobe Walls even though it was built out of sod and pickets.

It was not long before Charlie Rath came from Dodge City with a big wagon loaded with goods. He started a branch store to compete with Charlie Myers. Rath built a sod store smaller than Myers' just to the south of the saloon. Its doors were on the east and west ends of the small building.

They all built a stockade-type corral to provide safety for the many horses and mules. This cluster of picket and sod buildings soon became the hunters' headquarters.

The spring was unusually late that year; while the men waited for the buffalo, they loitered about Adobe Walls, ". . .joining in the fun that was rampant at that place. Our amusements were mostly card-playing, running horseraces, drinking whiskey, and shooting at targets," Mooar said.

Body of Ralph Morrison, killed and scalped near Fort Dodge, Kansas, in 1869.

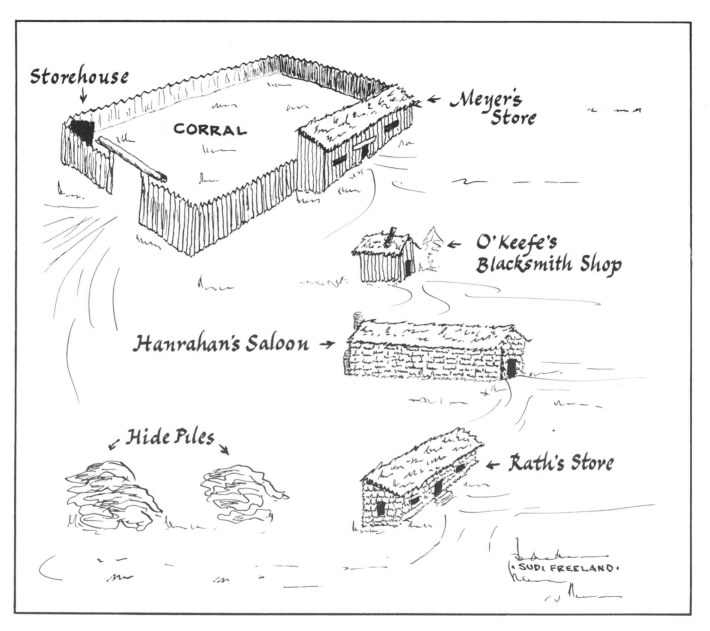

Storehouse

CORRAL

Meyer's Store

O'Keefe's Blacksmith Shop

Hanrahan's Saloon →

Hide Piles

← Rath's Store

· SUDI FREELAND ·

Sudi Freeland's drawing of Adobe Walls, the cluster of picket and sod buildings that served as headquarters for the hunters who headed south after buffalo in the Texas Panhandle.

The great herd came at last, and the hunters broke up into outfits. The gunmen killed all they could, working their skinners furiously to keep it. It was deadly business without any sentiment. Several parties were shot down by the Indians and scalped. But the hunters showed no intention of abandoning the range. The herds were at hand; prices were good. Business was good and the merchants sent back to Dodge City for a new stock of goods. Hide hunting was excellent and wagon trains headed north, groaning and creaking the 150 miles to Dodge City, overflowing with buffalo hides.

The Indians were never very far away. "Furthermore," commented Billy Dixon, "the buffaloes were becoming scarcer and scarcer each year, and it was expedient that we make hay while the sun shone. . . After all, it was not unusual to hear of two or three buffalo-hunters being scalped each year."

Hostile warriors, ones who killed and scalped on their raids down into Texas, began attacking isolated hide camps scattered about the Panhandle. They killed and mutilated Antelope Jack and Blue Billy on the Salt Fork of the Red River. They killed Tom Wallace and Dave Dudley, who were hunting with Joe Plummer, on the west side of White Deer Creek. Billy Dixon barely escaped with his life, but he lost his Big .50 Sharps.

Back at Adobe Walls the hunters gathered for safety, and for a few days, Hanrahan's saloon did a booming business. But, the call of the buffalo hide was too much, and buffalo were plentiful just a few miles out from Adobe Walls.

As the weather became truly Texan, the doors of the sod houses were left open at night to catch such breezes as there were and many of the men slept out of doors. There was no need to get up until late in the morning.

The Indian scare subsided, and most of the hunters no longer feared risking their scalps. They went out short distances to the north and east, since the Indians were off to the south. Back at Camp Supply, Indian Territory, post traders Lee and Reynolds heard rumors about a large force of Indians planning to attack Adobe Walls about June 27. The Indians on the southern plains were irritated and itching for a fight.

The heavy rains during the spring of 1874 had been especially hard on the Comanche. They were issued only half rations and were forced to butcher their horses and mules so as not to starve.

Plains Indians preparing for battl

A young Comanche brave, I-sa-tai (Little Wolf) claimed to have unusual powers. He brought the dead back to life and turned away bullets with his magic. Little Wolf told the Comanche the Great Spirit gave him a special message. They were not to follow the white man's ways, and they were to make war on whites, killing and scalping all palefaces.

The great medicine man became prominent among the Quahada Comanche. He ascended to the abode of a great spirit high above the heaven of the white man's Father, and there he learned to control the elements, to produce rain or cause drought; from his stomach he could bring forth as many cartridges as the Indians needed; and his black magic could so influence the guns of the white men that they could not shoot Indians.

The Comanche, now that their medicine man had made them invincible in battle, planned to kill the enemy tribe of the Tonkawa. But the commander of the Kiowa and Comanche Agency discovered the plan and the Tonkawa were removed to the protection of Fort Griffin.

The tribe was called together for a Sun Dance late in May. The Comancheros were on hand, with plenty of whiskey to add to the excitement and confusion. The tribes gathered on the bank of the Red River, and the chosen warriors spent four days building a special lodge for the dance. A freshly killed and stuffed painted buffalo was mounted atop the center pole of the lodge. "After we wipe out the white man," Little Wolf said, "the buffaloes will return from their hole in the earth in great numbers. The Great Spirit will be satisfied."

The dance lasted four days. It was expected to renew the powers of the tribe, assuring its success on the warpath and buffalo range. The Comanche sent out messengers and gathered many recruits. Special envoys carried the pipe of piece to the Cheyenne and Arapaho, the Kiowa and the Apache. The Comanche asked them to aid in destroying the hunters who were slaying the Indians' buffalo by the thousands.

The other tribes were equally eager. The attack on Adobe Walls was planned. Little Wolf, the inspired Comanche, prepared his medicine carefully. The doors of the houses would be open and the hunters would be charmed into sleep. The Indians would be daubed with war paint over which Little Wolf worked magic, and they would kill and scalp every buffalo hunter at Adobe Walls without the loss of a single brave.

A big feast was held and the Comanche recruited allies for help in the attack on the

Quanah Parker, the fierce rebel who led the Comanche in the attack on Adobe Walls. The two Indian maids beside him are believed to be his daughters.

buffalo hunters at Adobe Walls. Quanah Parker made strong talk to go along with the strong medicine of Little Wolf. Medicine arrows were passed out and nearly seven hundred warriors set out toward the frontier outpost. The Indian horsemen were ready for attack long before daylight.

Quanah Parker and Big Bow led two groups of Comanche, while Lone Wolf and Woman's Heart led the Kiowa. Stone Calf and White Shield led the Cheyenne. Little Wolf sat naked on his painted horse and said he was immune to the white man's bullets.

On the night of June 26-27, 1874, there were twenty-eight men and a woman who had come with her husband from Dodge City to open a restaurant at Adobe Walls. Twenty-five slept in the buildings, while two hunters and a Mexican bullwhacker slept in their wagons. There was no reason for alarm, even with only the sod-and-picket structures for a thin shell of protection. But a well-planned surprise attack could wipe out every man.

Jim Hanrahan was uneasy—it was 2:00 A.M. on June 27. This was the day for the savages to attack, if Amos Chapman's warning was true. The hills looked peaceful enough, but the Indians could be hiding. If they came, they would arrive ahead of sunrise. He fired a pistol into the night air and shouted, "Clear out! The ridge pole is breaking!"

Some of the men woke up and soon the commotion they made aroused others. Soon fifteen men were milling about the small saloon. It was only the ridge pole, not Indians. Hanrahan invited the hunters to have a free drink. A few stayed and had several, a few stayed awake and ate breakfast, but most went back to their bedrolls for a pre-dawn nap.

On the hills near Adobe Walls, the Indians waited for dawn. The medicine man was to be their chief in battle. He stood, naked except for a cap made of sage stems, to the right of the line, making his final invocations. Just as dawn was breaking, hundreds of warriors came charging toward the trading post. Terrifying war whoops split the early morning air.

Billy Dixon stood as if thunderstruck. He thought the Indians were going to run off the horses, so he raced out into the compound to save his prize saddlehorse. Then he saw the warriors were riding straight toward the buildings. They were not after horses, they were after paleface scalps.

By now, the hunters at Adobe Walls were wide awake. Some were barefoot, some 128 wore only their underwear, but they knocked out windows and hastily built a barricade.

The hundreds of warriors, the flower of the fighting men of the southwestern plains tribes mounted upon their finest horses, armed with guns and lances, and carrying heavy shields of thick buffalo hide, were coming like the wind. Over all was splashed the rich colors of red, vermilion, and ochre—on the bodies of the men, on the running horses. Scalps dangled from bridles; gorgeous war bonnets fluttered their plumes; bright feathers dangled from the tails and manes of the horses. But each of the fourteen guns in Adobe Walls was loaded and waiting.

The Sadler Brothers and their big shepherd dog were sleeping in one of their wagons. They failed to hear the attacking Indians, so early in the fight they and the dog were killed. The Comanche lifted the dog's hair right along with the hair of the Sadlers. The other defenders gave a good account of themselves, for they were all crack shots.

The Indians swarmed about the two houses and the saloon. Their magic would surely protect them; so they fought without fear, taking no care for their lives and charging directly to the doors of the buildings. As the defenders of Adobe Walls shot from the portholes, they placed the muzzles of their guns on the very faces of the savages.

For two hours the Indians made an incessant assault, battering the doors of one building partly open, but not effecting an entrance. Riderless horses dashed back and forth through the bombardment of guns, lances, and arrows.

During the first attack, one Comanche and two Cheyenne were shot. One of the Cheyenne warriors was the son of Chief Stone Calf. Many warriors tried to rescue the wounded. Chief Quanah Parker raced in on his mount, grabbed the young warrior, and carried him back to safety. All of the horses and oxen lay dead in the corral. They were easy marks for the Indian sharpshooter and soon their bodies began to bloat in the summer sun.

"At one time there was a lull in the fight," Bob Wright later recalled. "There was a young warrior, more daring and desperate than his fellows, mounted on a magnificent pony, decorated with a gaudy war bonnet, and his other apparel equally as brilliant. He wanted, perhaps, to gain distinction for his bravery and become a great chief of his tribe and made a bold dash from among his companions toward the buildings. He rode with the speed of an eagle, and as straight as an arrow, for the side of the building where the portholes were most numerous and danger greatest, succeeded in reaching them, and leaping from his horse, pushed his six-shooter through a porthole and emptied it, filling the room with smoke. He then attempted a retreat, but in a moment he was shot down; he staggered to his feet, but was again shot down, and whilst lying on the ground, he deliberately drew another pistol from his belt and blew out his brains."

Billy Tyler was wounded when he went to help the horses in the picket stockade, and died within an hour. By ten o'clock the attacks were less frequent, for the Indians learned they could not gain entrance to the fortified building. Also, the Indians were disappointed, and worried over their mounting casualties. Little Wolf, the prophet, was bad medicine!

In the afternoon the Indians made another assault. They left a field strewn with dead horses and dead Indians. They killed one buffalo hunter, and another was killed when the hammer of his gun struck an obstruction and the accidental discharge tore into his head.

Chief Quanah Parker was wounded and his horse was shot out from under him. Little Wolf was disgraced for life. His promises were false. The white man's bullets killed brave warriors. Seven Cheyenne and five Comanche lay dead or dying on the plain. Twenty-eight oxen and fifty-six horses were dead at the small trading post. Four of the hide hunters were killed that day.

The Indians finally rode off, but danger was not far away. The hunters left and Adobe Walls was abandoned. Late in the fall, the Indians burned the remaining buildings, glad to be rid of the disgraceful symbol. The attack on Adobe Walls was not the massacre Little Wolf had promised. Yet, for over a year, the Texas Panhandle was free from the commercial hide hunter.

Thirty-eight years later, the disgraced medicine man, living at Fort Sill, avowed that the outcome of the battle of Adobe Walls had not been the fault of his medicine. On the morning after the Indians started out, some Cheyenne killed a skunk and so shattered the force of his magic.

The hunters were escorted back to Dodge City, some ten days after the battle, by three companies of cavalry. General Miles was assigned to head an expedition against the Indian bands in the Adobe Walls district.

The Last of the Great Herds

Colonel MacKenzie, with seven troops of the Fourth Cavalry and five companies of the Tenth Infantry, went looking for the Comanche in September of 1874. The band led by Chief Quanah Parker was encamped in Pala Dura Canyon. This is a deep *barranca* found by Coronado in 1541, and its rugged walls and steep bluffs made a fine hiding place for the hundreds of tepees.

At dawn on September 27, MacKenzie attacked the village in full force. Indian women and children ran screaming about in the confusion. The colonel burned all the tepees and destroyed a large supply of winter meat and provisions. He ordered fourteen hundred horses and mules killed. The only casualty among the soldiers was a wounded bugler. There were four Indians killed during the raid.

The loss of tepees, food, and horses was a severe blow to the Comanche. They walked sheepishly back to their reservation in Indian Territory.

Now that the hostile Indians were gone from western Texas, the hide hunters started out from the Texas frontier towns. The Texas headquarters of the hide hunters was Fort Griffin, located on the Clear Fork of the Brazos River.

By the fall of 1874 the village, situated on a flat below the fort, was a popular outpost. There were three stores, three saloons, and a couple of sporting houses. Wood choppers, freighters, wolf hunters, and a few hardy families lived there. It was in the very heart of the Texas herd of buffalo.

To play safe, the hide hunters worked in large outfits. The Mooar brothers left Dodge City in a party with ten other hunters and a dozen wagons. They headed south, deep into the heartland of Texas, where they hunted in the valley of the Brazos River northwest of Fort Griffin and found an abundance of shaggies. By November, 1875, they collected over four thousand hides, all dry and ready to sell. They loaded the hides and headed for

Denison, Texas, where they sold the entire lot. After buying several months' supplies, they headed back to the Fort Griffin area.

Early spring of 1876 found Wright and John Mooar busy as ever. Bills of sale saved by the two brothers showed that they had sold 30 pounds of buffalo meat at 6¢ a pound and 164 tongues at 20¢ apiece at Fort Griffin. They bought sugar, canned tomatoes, four skillets, yeast powder, molasses, and a keg of nails. During the month of April, they sold 450 choice hides. These were extra good ones, suitable for making into fancy buffalo robes.

Fort Griffin was where the hide hunter felt most at home. It was the toughest town on the Texas frontier. Merchants sold guns, ammunition, as well as camp supplies, while they in turn bought flint hides to ship by wagon to the railroad at Forth Worth. The town was filled with hastily built saloons, gambling halls, dance halls, and bagnios. Day and night, the streets echoed with whoops and curses of cowboys, bullwhackers, hide hunters, off-duty soldiers, and Indians.

The dance halls were notorious. J. W. Woody, a greenhorn from Missouri, remarked, "I saw men and women dancing together without a stitch of clothing on." There were plenty of soiled doves in the small frontier town. Lotty, Mollie, Minnie, and Long Kate all ran houses of sin.

Money flowed freely at Fort Griffin. Frank Conrad reported he sold $4,000 worth of merchandise in one day, $2,500 of which was for guns and ammunition alone. One buffalo hunter came into town, sold his season's kill for $1,500, and by the next morning was forced to borrow money for breakfast.

The demand for ammunition was great. Conrad frequently kept 30 tons of lead and 5 tons of black powder stored in his warehouse and magazine. The flint hides poured into Fort Griffin in great numbers and prices went down. Even at $1.25 per hide, 200,000 hides sold during the winter of 1876-77 brought in $250,000.

In the railroad town of Fort Worth, hide wagons were as common as trail herds of Longhorn cattle. The Fort Worth *Democrat* of May 3, 1877 reported: "A train of ten wagons arrived from the west. In front were eleven yokes of oxens, driven by one man and dragging after them four large new wagons, each heavily laden with hides. Two other teams, with seven yokes of oxen each, drawing three wagons, followed. There probably were twenty-five hundred to three thousand hides in the train."

crumbling walls of the Fort Griffin post sutler's store.

Later in August the same paper noted, "There are 60,000 baled hides piled high on a platform, along the Texas and Pacific Railroad tracks."

The carnage on the southern plains reached its peak in 1873. The white hunters alone were shipping more than a million hides a year. According to the ratio of one hide to every two animals killed, these hides must have accounted for approximately 2 million buffalo.

Considering the great number of hunters on the range and the quantity of animals they killed, it is strange that by the close of the 1873 season, the white hunters were puzzled by the scarcity of buffalo. With the increase in hunters and the noticeable decrease in the number of animals, more of the total product was saved. In 1874, one railroad shipped more than a million and a half pounds of meat where none was carried the year before.

By the close of the hunting season of 1875, the southern herd was completely gone. The season of 1876 saw the incredulous hunters outfit expensive expeditions and set forth to the empty, bone-littered hunting grounds, then return empty-handed in the fall. Disbelief was prevalent everywhere. They had accomplished the impossible, the total annihilation of millions of animals.

With the extermination of the buffalo south of the Platte, a period of bewilderment seized upon the army of hunters, and a few seasons of comparative inaction lay across the desolated pastureland. Then the Northern Pacific began building its line into the range of the northern herd. In 1881, there was the same kind of stampede in that direction the southern range had witnessed just ten years before.

The hide hunters were, of course, not really interested in the buffalo meat. They did save the tongue, which was smoked over a small fire of buffalo chips and green twigs. The rest of the animal they left for the wolves.

Several farmers in eastern Texas took a different view of this waste. They saw an opportunity for a large profit, and drove a great herd of hogs out to the buffalo range. They filled their wagons with buffalo meat and hides, and their hogs fattened on the carcasses. They drove the hogs back home, slaughtered them, and got top prices for the extra-fine pork!

By 1878 Fort Griffin showed signs of civilization, with two hotels, the Southern and the Planters. A stone school building was completed in August and a Masonic Lodge started in September.

*One of the dugouts used by the intrepid buffalo
hunters of the snow-bound northern plains.*

Very few hide men went on to the Texas range in the winter of 1878-79. They found barely enough buffalo to make hunting pay. The Mooar brothers reported, "We had a little success, but the Texas hide business was fading fast away."

The hunt was much smaller; the buffalo seemed to be moving northward out of Texas. As the hide hunters drifted away from Fort Griffin, they followed the trail north to check on reports of a large herd still grazing in Montana. Fort Griffin felt the loss of the hide business. Within but a few years it was a ghost town.

The hunt for hides moved far north. The intervening lull in the supply of hides sent the price up to three times the best figure received during the southern hunt. By 1882, there were five thousand hunters on the far northern range. These hunters, profiting by their experience in the south, exterminated the northern herd much more rapidly and efficiently.

The hunting season of 1883 finished off the northern herd. A few small bands scattered into the hills and rough country where pursuit was difficult. They no longer felt safety in numbers, nor did they mill about stupidly when fired upon. At the first sign of danger, the small bands would scatter and disappear as successfully as quail in a cornfield. The endangered buffalo

now chose to make his last stand upon the terrain where he could outdistance any horse. His final extinction here was due, again, to the still hunt of his foe and the long-range rifle.

On the northern plains, there were still good stands of buffalo, and the hide hunter could pull down fifty to sixty buffalo a day. The railroad was nearby. The Northern Pacific Railroad reached the rough and ready town of Miles City, Montana, during the early part of 1880, which encouraged the hunters. It was a way to send a lot of hides back to the eastern markets. It made the northern ranges safer, for a railroad brought in settlers, and the Army was forced to give them protection from Indian raids. Custer and the Seventh Cavalry were wiped out at the Little Big Horn in 1876, and this forced the Army to chase Chief Sitting Bull's savage Sioux and teach them a real lesson. The boom of the Big .50 was frequent on the northern ranges, and Miles City grew to several blocks of cabins, stores, and honky-tonks.

The *Yellowstone Journal,* in February, 1881, reported: "In January more than a hundred local citizens went out after hides, and these are worth a dollar and a half apiece. There are more than four thousand hides on hand in the storerooms of one of our local firms. Other traders have almost as many."

138

A pair of buffalo grazing against a backdrop of snowcaps.

Sitting Bull, Sioux Indian Chief who, with Rain-in-the-Face, led his tribe at the battle of the Little Big Horn.

Most of the killing in the winter of 1880-81 was in the triangle formed by the Missouri, Musselshell, and Yellowstone rivers. Prime hides were bringing an average of $2.70, and over 200,000 were shipped east during the season (December-March). Seventy-five thousand hides went down the Missouri River on flat-bottomed, sternwheeler steamboats; the rest went by rail.

The improved Sharps rifles with telescopic sights gave a hunter a good point of vantage, and he could keep a distant herd milling indefinitely simply by picking off any bulls seeking to lead the herd away. Hides were worth more now—$2.00 to $3.50; and there was not so much of the waste that had characterized the southern hunt. Every hundred hides carried to market represented not more than one hundred and ten dead buffalo. In Kansas ten years before, that many hides represented at least two hundred buffalo. Much of the meat of these northern buffalo was saved and marketed, as well.

The winter hunting caused a large part of the herd to move eastward into the Dakotas, where the Indians came out in large numbers to satisfy their need for meat, robes, and hides. They even hunted to sell to a white trader for guns and firewater. The Shoshone sold over two thousand robes and hides to the traders at Fort Washakie. The return of the buffalo to their former grazing grounds was good news to the Indians.

It also brought many a hide hunter into the area. It was estimated that during the winter of 1881-82 over five thousand whites were shooting and skinning on the northern plains. These hunters made record killings: John Edwards shot seventy-five shaggies in a single stand, and Doc Zahl brought down eighty-five. Vick Smith claimed he bagged 107 buffalo in a little over an hour, without ever moving from his first shooting site. Later, he claimed he killed five thousand buffalo that winter.

During the entire season of 1881-82—the biggest for the northern region—one Montana dealer, H. F. Douglas, shipped 250,000 hides. The big kill was the result of deep snows and severe cold, for snow made it hard for the buffalo to escape the marksman, and the remaining animals were pushed into smaller bunches.

Joseph Ullman, the New York furrier, gave William T. Hornaday, who was investigating on behalf of the National Museum, these figures: "In 1881 we handled about 14,000 hides," he said, "average cost about $3.50, and 12,000 robes, average cost about $7.50. In 1882

Rain-in-the-Face, Sioux chief who also fought Custer.

we purchased between 35,000 and 40,000 hides, at an average cost of about $3.50 and about 10,000 robes, at an average cost of $8.50. In 1883 we purchased from 6,000 to 7,000 hides and about 1,500 to 2,000 robes at a slight advance in price."

The Messrs. Moskowitz, furriers of New York and Chicago, purchased 35,000 robes and 4,500 hides in 1880; and 23,350 robes and 26,000 hides in 1881, at a total cost for these two years of over $430,000. In 1882 and 1883, buying as many robes and hides as they could, and paying higher prices, the sum of their payments for robes and hides was under $157,000.

The winter of 1882-83 marked the last hunt on the northern ranges. Only a fraction of the buffalo were left. The largest herd was estimated at seventy-five thousand; smaller bunches were reported scattered here and there throughout the Montana Territory. Only a few shipments of hides trickled down from the trading posts, and shipments of robes and hides by the carload were a thing of the past.

By 1883 the day of the hide hunter had ended. The hunters went back to their farms, or started herding cattle. The Longhorns from Texas took over the buffalo ranges of Montana.

The decline of the buffalo, in the years from 1840 to 1889, was paralleled by tremendous progress in rifle design. Improvements came thick and fast. The breech-loading rifle, invented by John H. Hall and greatly improved by Sharps, Remington, and other manufacturers, opened the door for the elongated bullet. That bullet, in turn, speeded the development of the modern cartridge. And the cartridge led to the development of the repeating rifle.

Until 1840, the overwhelming majority of riflemen used the muzzle loader and the round ball. That combination had definite limitations, however, in both accuracy and striking power, and especially at ranges beyond two hundred or three hundred yards. Small balls were more accurate; big, heavy ones had more killing power. The problem was to combine the two virtues. The solution was fairly obvious—some form of elongated bullet with small diameter, yet plenty of weight.

The first Sharps really gave them their start. Since it was no longer necessary to load through the muzzle, a man could use a slightly oversized conical bullet that would engage the rifling in the barrel. The Sharps utilized such a bullet in a "cartridge," a crude paper tube containing black powder in one end and the bullet in the other. When the action was closed, after loading, the ascending breechblock sheared the paper tail off the cartridge and exposed

141

the powder for the percussion flash. Later, Sharps marketed a linen cartridge, which was even more dependable.

The first "complete" cartridge—one containing bullet, powder, and priming compound—was pioneered by Smith and Wesson in 1859. It was a rimfire, not unlike the one used in today's .22 caliber rifles. S. & W. made the old percussion cap the base of its new cartridge; when the firing pin pinched the rim of the base, it set off the primer—fulminate of mercury, which in turn fired the powder.

The S. & W. cartridge had a major defect—its case was made of soft copper, which was not safe with heavy loads. But another big improvement was on the way. In 1869, Colonel Henry Berdan devised a practical method of "drawing" brass—forming strong, seamless cases from solid metal. Brass proved almost the ideal material for cartridge making. It was elastic, expanding just enough under an explosion to help seal in powder gases—up to that time quite a problem in breechloaders.

The modern cartridge was born. Two other great firearms developments were to follow in short order—the repeating rifle and smokeless powder. By this time, all that remained of the millions of buffalo were their whitening bones on the prairie.

The bison shed his mass instincts and became an alert, thinking animal too late for the survival of his kind in the wild state. He disappeared completely from even the most remote areas within the next few years. Of all those millions, less than five hundred bison survived to progenerate the species. This small number has given us the captive bison we shelter in our zoos and parks today.

143

udy in light and shadow as a bison herd
s across the Montana range in the late
noon sun.

The Buffalo Come Home

Now only the bones strewn on the Great Plains told where the buffalo had once lived. The hide hunter, the wolf, the vulture, rot and decay had done their damage. In many places where the hide men had once made their stands, buffalo bones made the prairie white for miles and miles. These bones were both nuisance and godsend to the prairie sodbuster.

Eventually, even the bones of the buffalo were picked. In 1872, it was observed that one old settler drove his team and empty wagon out onto the prairie every single day. He would return each night to the Dodge City siding of the Santa Fe with a load of old buffalo bones.

"What the hell is that old nithead doing?" jeered one of the locals.

"He's just touched in the head," answered another saloon bum.

"Piling up a heap of bones is a silly-looking occupation to me," voiced a third.

But the old man continued to do so. Ridicule and even the nickname "Old Buffalo Bones" did not stop him. One fine day, the citizens of Dodge were surprised to see some empty boxcars switched onto the siding, and "Old Buffalo Bones" loading the freight cars from his pile. The engine hooked on, and puffed its way off to the East. The word spread around town. "Old Bones" received eight dollars a ton for those damned old, whitened relics. In no time at all his neighbors became bone pickers, too, and whole train loads were being shipped back East to the fertilizer factories and made into potash.

The falling farm prices of 1872, along with the drought and grasshoppers, had brought the fringe settlements to near starvation. The "fool hoe-man," as the cowboys called him, found buffalo bones a God-sent blessing. The sodbuster could load his wagon with them, drive into town, and trade the load for the necessities of life.

Fertilizing plants bought the bones to make into phosphates; sugar refineries bought the bones for carbon. The gathering of buffalo bones became a regular industry as early as

145

from the plains.

A grim reminder. A heap of buffalo bones, mostly skulls, at Langdon in Alberta, Canada.

1872, when the farmers followed the buffalo butchers into the ranges that had just been devastated; over 1 million pounds were shipped on the Santa Fe that year. In 1873, the Santa Fe carried over 2 million pounds of buffalo bones, and in 1874—when the hunters followed the buffalo below the Cimarron, and the "fool hoe-men" were rapidly claiming Kansas for their own—the railroad shipped east almost 7 million tons of buffalo bones.

"Buffalo bones are legal tender in Dodge City" was a common newspaper quip in 1874. There were great stacks, hundreds of tons of bones, piled up beside the Santa Fe track. Bone stacks towered above the boxcars; and often there were not enough cars to move them.

John Cook saw a huge rick of buffalo bones on the Santa Fe railroad right-of-way, and twenty miles ahead, another on the track from Granada, Colorado. Piles twelve feet high, nearly that wide at the base and one-half-mile long were common. The usual price was seven to ten dollars a ton.

Without the buffalo bones, many an early homesteader on the plains would have gone back East a total failure. The bone gatherers followed closely after the hide hunters. Sometimes, they even got ahead of the railroad builders and left their piles of bones along the future right-of-way.

Freight trains carried supplies west and hauled bones to the carbon works in St. Louis. The new bones were used in sugar refining, the old weather-beaten ones were ground up and made into fertilizer, and a few choice specimens went to England for fine bone china. Even the horns were valuable, and the early sodbuster could sell them for 1½¢ a pound. They also served as the raw material for buttons, combs, and knife handles.

The bone gatherers had a song:

> Wagons pull in from the prairie dry,
> To ricks of bleaching bones piled high.
> Four dollars a ton—but not for Sed,
> A rattler was watching that buffalo head.
> One settler less to tear up sod
> And pray for rain from a deaf old God.

In 1870, the buffalo herds had interfered with the pleasure of hunting, whether antelope, deer, or game birds—even with hunting the buffalo themselves. Now, in 1871, the hunter had to go perhaps a hundred miles south and west to find respectable shooting. It was true there was still the great Texas herd, but there were Kiowa and Comanche down there. Compared to them, the Sioux and Cheyenne sending a few arrows and bullets into a camp as they loped past were like the sky pilots spouting hellfire on Dodge's Front Street of a Saturday night. But now it was go south, or pick bones and fight off the hungry settlers to get them.

And then Dodge City received the news of Black Friday and the crash of Jay Cook's railroad empire. For the next few weeks, there was much uneasy talk around Dodge. All

the hide sheds and corrals were empty, and the stores piled high with goods ordered for a big winter that brought in very little money. Bones, instead of hides, became the legal tender of Dodge now—bones at six to ten dollars a ton. More than 1 million pounds of bones went east on the Santa Fe that year. This would be multiplied many times over by 1874.

Dodge City, the progeny of the hide men, was deserted by them now, for all the world to see. Still, as a dutiful father might buy his daughter a bolt of calico now and then until her new husband could keep her clothed, she got a little continuing buffalo trade through such men as Rath, Reynolds, and the Mooars.

But, as the new hide towns moved deeper into Texas, Fort Worth became a nearer, handier outlet. It was already a gathering place for buyers. As early as 1873-74, there had been public auctions of hides there, with perhaps as many as two hundred thousand sold to the highest bidders in one or two days.

With the trickle of buffalo business, Dodge managed to survive the panic in the East. She survived the drought, too, and the grasshoppers—a shabby little border town of weathering false fronts, some with barrels of water on the roof to tip over if a fire burned through, and at least slow its spread through the tinder-dry streets.

The railroad, its rails rusting, was stalled two years at the Colorado line. Then, in the spring of 1875 when the railroad began building again, Dodge was the nearest frontier metropolis on payday. There was still a large bone business, although much of the picking was by settlers. A ragged drylander might haul in a load of bones as he had once filled his wagon with butter, eggs, and garden truck back East. Some traders made a big business out of buffalo bones, buying them up at $2.50 a ton on the range, and getting eight to ten dollars at the railroad, sometimes swelling the profit a little by watering the sunbaked midsummer pick, just as the beaver traders once rubbed sand into the fur when the hides sold by the pound.

Many a farmer who lost his crop kept the family alive on his proceeds from buffalo bones. Under the influence of former hunters and freighters, a kind of order came to the business. A bone man selected a promising location, perhaps a flat of short mesquite grass dotted white, or a long grass bottom full of darker, taller, fertilized spots where carcasses had rotted. He gathered his bones into great piles that looked like reluctant snowdrifts left

149

"Curing Hide and Bones," from the April 4, 1874 issue of HARPER'S WEEKLY.

behind by a plains blizzard, each ton of bones representing approximately one hundred dead buffalo. These piles were entirely the picker's property, as though he had paid taxes on them, and they were usually left strictly alone, although on the public domain. Later, he hauled them in to the ricks growing along the railroad at all the jerkwater stations, some a mile long, to wait for an empty eastbound freight train.

Over in Montana, most of the hunters who outfitted the fall of 1883 as usual, spending many thousands of dollars, found nothing but bones and very hungry swarms of buffalo gnats. They came back bankrupt and finally drifted into mining, cowboying, or followed the road agent and outlaw to Robbers' Roost or half a dozen other hideouts.

Even the bone ricks along the last railroad to tap the hide country—the Northern Pacific—began to shrink until there were only a few loads, brought in by settlers to trade for coffee and calico and shoes against the long, hard winters.

Bones had been going out ever since the railroad came. M. I. McCreight, former bone buyer, told of a pile at the west end of Devil's Lake, Dakota Territory, which contained 250 carloads or 2,125 tons, with another 150 carloads at the southern shore, and a pile of 300 at Mouse River. Fred Stoltz, who bought buffalo bones, once had 400 or 500 carloads on hand when the prices fell. In dry years the farmers lived off the bones they brought to Minot, at about $20.00 a load, some accounts say; others put the price at $7.00 or $8.00 a load. Not all loads were alike; perhaps the $20.00 was paid for those hauled in the high, slatted bone racks of the time.

Indians, too, began to pick up the last remains of the buffalo, and instead of burning the prairie to crowd a herd closer together in a surround, they burned it now to show up the bones, although this cut their value. An advertisement by Bickett and Foote, 1000 TONS OF BONES WANTED, ran in the Dickinson (Dakota) *Press* the spring of 1884. The June 27 issue said, ". . . 77 yoke of oxen brought in bones yesterday" and that ". . . 34 yoke arrived from Deadwood loaded with bones." Dickinson, just east of the big herd, was a main outfitting point for hunters, and now it was cleaning up on the leavings.

One bone-buying firm estimated that over the seven years, 1884-1891, they bought the bones of approximately 5,950,000 buffalo skeletons, and there were many firms in the business. The Topeka *Mail and Breeze*, speaking of "the extinct industry, bones," said:

A "real good time" at the turn of the century. Many hunters became rodeo cowboys once the great herds were decimated.

"Allowing forty feet for a car, it would have made a string of cars seven thousand, five hundred and seventy-five miles long, enough to more than fill two tracks from New York to San Francisco."

The records show that, during the years from 1868 to 1881, over $2,500,000 worth of buffalo bones were shipped east from the state of Kansas, and other states profited as well. Hundreds and hundreds of tons were piled along the right-of-way in bone ricks taller than boxcars. With the dry air of Kansas, it took a hell of a lot of bones to make a ton. Throwing water over a load would reportedly increase the weight 25 percent.

A few freighters on the Santa Fe Trail hauled bones to Dodge City, while the Santa Fe built a separate siding for loading. The railroad provided special cars that could be loaded from the top because of buffalo bones that came from as far away as Texas.

The Texas and Pacific Railroad was building west from Fort Worth, and as it penetrated the Texas grasslands it gave rise to many new towns. Each became an important shipping point for bones: Blair, Abilene, Colorado City, Sweet Water, and Albany all got their start as bone-sidings.

A freight train from Abilene, Texas, to New Orleans in 1880, with a full complement of boxcars, carried nothing but buffalo bones. A fancy price was paid; the news spread; and bone haulers flocked into the Panhandle and eastern Colorado. Prairie fires had destroyed millions of pounds before the salvagers came, but the business lasted for nearly two years. The markets were glutted; but the average price for a ton of buffalo bones delivered at the railway station did not fall below six dollars.

The wagons loaded high with white remains stood in the streets, and the buyers went from one wagon to another, bidding on the contents. The average price was still eight dollars a ton, or about three dollars a wagonload. Later on, when bones became scarce, the price rose to twenty-one dollars a ton. The bone boom seldom lasted over two or three years in any one area. Yet, bone gathering continued on a small scale for a decade or so.

Although the railroad was a long way from the buffalo range of Indian Territory, hundreds of wagon loads of bones were hauled from Oklahoma country to Wichita. Freighters returning with empty wagons, after dropping their goods at the military posts or the Indian agencies, stopped in the Cimarron Valley, or near the Salt Fork, and loaded their wagons

153

piles along the railroad bed.

high with buffalo bones to make the return trip profitable.

Indians began to pick up the last remains of their cattle. In the spring of 1884, bone gathering began on a large scale up north. In the Dakotas, the Indians gathered and hauled most of the bones into the frontier towns. M. I. McCreight recalled that, when he was about twenty, he worked for a small Dakota bank. His principal duty was to buy the bones the Indians offered for sale.

"In the distance the townsmen could see the wagon trains of the Indians as they followed the winding trails leading over the prairies toward the market. Out in front," wrote McCreight, "stood the chief of the tribe, his long black hair plaited in braids and a blanket draped over his shoulder. The chief was followed by a motley array of men, women, children, and dogs. Most of the men rode on ponies, but others came afoot. Their approach was marked by much cracking of whips and the screeching of the wood car wheels, which were in sad need of grease. The dogs yelped and snapped at each other as the caravan slowly approached the town.

"About a half mile outside of the small town, the Indians stopped and unloaded their tepees. They made camp; then the chief and his council walked into town. They asked in a very solemn manner what price was being paid for bones.

"I told them the rate was six dollars a ton," wrote McCreight, "But no matter what price was offered, they went back to their camp and brought in their loaded carts to be weighed. From the scales they drove the carts to the railroad siding and unloaded. The minute they received the money the Indians swarmed into the local stores to spend it. Only after they spent their last thin dime, they would break camp and leave town."

By 1888, the Great Plains were cleared of buffalo bones, except for a few left down in Indian Territory. The boomers, who showed up wherever there was trade, and sooners in search of land to claim brought hundreds of wagonloads from down below the Cimarron to Dodge and Liberal. Some they gathered in No Man's Land, and others they gathered farther down in the Territory. One of the first things a sooner did after building a sod house was to load his wagons with old bones and haul them to Kansas.

Julian Ralph and a friend were traveling westward in Canada on the Canadian Pacific in 1888. "As we journeyed on we found that the bison's remains had been made the basis of

The few surviving buffalo were hunted down relentle
ly. Museums, circuses, and breeders bid high for the

a thriving business. At the outset we saw a few bison bones dotting the grass in white specks here and there, and soon we met great trains, each of many boxcars, laden with nothing but these weather-whitened relics. Presently we came to stations where, beside the tracks, mounds of these bones were heaped up and rude men were swelling the heaps with wagonloads garnered far from the railroad, for a great business has grown up collecting these trophies. For years the business of carting them away has gone on."

The gathering of the many trainloads of bones, and their weathering, left no visible reminder of the millions of buffalo that had roamed the plains a few years earlier. The live buffalo were so scarce in 1886 that the National Museum in Washington, D. C., experienced a great deal of difficulty finding a suitable prime specimen for their mounted exhibit.

In the spring of 1886, the directors of the National Museum decided to exhibit a mounted group of buffalo, "a small square patch from the wildest part of the wild west." But the museum found almost no presentable specimens. The chief taxidermist discovered, after extensive correspondence, that the destruction of all the large herds, outside the remote, snowbound range in northern Canada, was an accomplished fact. The taxidermist was William T. Hornaday.

Later, a man in New Hampshire and another in Oklahoma were to render timely, vital service in the preservation of the buffalo; but the pioneer labor and inspiration of Mr. Hornaday makes the rescue of the buffalo from extermination a personal achievement for him. When the hide hunters cleared the plains for the cattleman and simplified the Indian problem, they came close to wiping out one of North America's most impressive animals.

Admirably suited to the extremes of heat and cold, storm and drought of the Great Plains, the American bison is also the only furbearing member of the bovine species. This fur the Indians used to line their babies' cradles and to weave blankets, very much as the Navajo does with wool today. Our own cattle, probably derived from a cross between the small Asiatic bison and the large European bison some six thousand years ago, were well adapted to Europe's climate, but under the rigorous conditions in North America they died in droves.

For the past 250 years, individual stock raisers of the United States and Canada have observed the rugged qualities of this indigenous American animal and worked for a successful cross between the bison and domestic cattle. They sought to combine the hairiness of the

157

The buffalo's thick coat of fur distinguishes him from his bovine cousins.

bison with the beef qualities of the domestic breed. Many men spent their fortunes and the greater parts of their lives in the effort.

It was often said the buffalo were too wild and intractable ever to be confined within fences. While there is no question the bison was a very wild and powerful animal, all of them alive today are contained within fences. Good strong fences, to be sure. It was believed they could not be domesticated, yet, as early as the year 1700, men of patience broke them to the yoke, where they proved faster and stronger than oxen. The erroneous beliefs concerning bison are legion. However, the most common reason for discouragement in the efforts to tame and crossbreed them with domestic cattle is the high percentage of sterility in the hybrid off-spring—especially among the males.

Typical examples of men who spent a great deal of time in the struggle to develop a successful breed from this cross were S. L. Bedson of Manitoba, Canada, Colonel Charles Goodnight, the Texan cattle king, and C. J. Jones of Garden City, Kansas. The combined experience of these three men covered a period of about fifty years.

In 1888, Kansas breeder "Buffalo" Jones purchased the Bedson herd for fifty thousand

A quartet of buffalo, carefully chosen for experimental breeding with domestic cattle, play on a northern preserve.

dollars—a far cry from the hide price of the recent past when buffalo were killed just for the fun of it. However, the dreams and labors of Jones met the same fate as others of his day and his herd of strange-looking cattle of many shapes, sizes, and colors was finally sold for beef and robes. Many attribute to him and to Goodnight the name by which the longed-for breed has become known, the "cattalo."

The alarmists who had predicted the extinction of the American bison found receptive ears. "Only 250 living buffalo are left on the face of the earth," they said. A little careful investigation placed the figure higher. Nearly a thousand were found. On December 8, 1905, a group of sixteen men met in the Lion House of the Bronx Park Zoo, and they organized The American Bison Society. The first activity of this group was to make a census of the living buffalo in the United States.

Martin S. Garretson was chosen, for he had worked as a cowboy at the Goodnight Ranch in the Texas Panhandle. Experienced, wise to the cattle trails and western ranches, he traveled far and wide over the Great Plains. He found 835 wild buffalo, and 256 in captivity. A few wild buffalo had wandered into Yellowstone Park and were being protected from poachers; others were scattered in isolated valleys. There was a rumor of how the wild buffalo were reduced in number to fifty. Surely this was much, much too close to complete extinction. At last some energetic men went to work.

Mr. Hornaday was doubly alarmed. He still had no good group for the museum, and the noblest beast of the western world—only recently the most numerous ruminant known—was in immediate danger of extinction. He finally got his specimen in its finest pelage in December of 1886.

Colonel Goodnight reported he saw a buffalo stampede that split a herd of thirteen hundred cattle right smack in two. This herd was being driven by Goodnight to the Pecos River. Luckily, his cowboys were about equally divided on each side of the herd when the charging bison crashed through. Hard riding on the part of his cowboys finally brought the two parts of the herd of Longhorns back together; but, for the next hundred miles, it took constant attention and alertness to prevent a mix-up between Goodnight's Longhorns and the buffalo.

161   Colonel Goodnight is the man who salvaged a portion of the buffalo in the eighteen-

eighties, when there was grave danger of complete destruction of all the southern herds. At his wife's suggestion he had started a herd on his ranch near the present city of Amarillo. He captured several wild calves, a male and a female, and his cowboys roped others. Gradually, the herd increased. This helped save the buffalo from complete extinction.

The colonel was an amateur cattle breeder and was constantly trying to improve his herds of Texas Longhorns. In order to do this, he bred his prize bulls to buffalo cows, and a better buffalo bull to several of his prize cows. The cross resulted in an odd-looking group of beasts. His herd of buffalo gradually became less and less pure blood, due to the many experimental crosses.

Finally, in the early nineteen-hundreds, to get a pure strain of buffalo it was necessary to bring bulls from the New York Zoological Gardens into the Wichita Wildlife Preserve in Oklahoma. This was quite a chore; but it did result in the present herd of buffalo that is today grazing peacefully in the Wichita Mountains of southwestern Oklahoma.

The Wichita National Bison Herd was founded in 1907, from a total of fifteen head of buffalo given by the Zoological Society. There were four distinct blood lines in the group of four bulls, six adult cows, one spike bull, two young cows, a bull calf, and a female calf. The naturalists worried about Texas fever, and all fifteen animals were sprayed with a crude oil mixture. They liked the range on the Wichita Wild Life Preserve and flourished.

A few hundred buffalo are in Yellowstone National Park and there is a herd on the Flathead Reservation in Montana. Wind Cave National Park in the Black Hills has perhaps the largest herd of buffalo today. There are scattered herds in various other parks and a few in private herds.

In 1916, the Canadian Government took up the fight on behalf of those who believed in the "cattalo"—the breed that existed only in the minds of men. In subsequent years the men at the Dominion Experimental Farms have disproved many, and confirmed few, of the theories concerning the bison and crossbreeding. The Canadians are doing a great work quietly. They are making no boasts or promises, and they do not like the frequent newspaper and magazine articles stating unequivocally that the true breed of "cattalo" is now achieved.

Recently the men most closely identified with the project stated:

162

In the Wichita Mountains Wildlife Refuge in Cache, Oklaho
a bison herd moves along the hillside. Note the numerous cal

The stock we have obtained thus far cannot be called a distinct breed. The most one can expect is a type. If by selection and judicious mating one succeeds in fixing that type, then one has a breed. These young animals in the pasture will form the nucleus from which we hope to

Buffalo Jones rescues two buffalo calves from a pack of wolves.

At the height of the buffalo destruction, Army men would hold shooting contests. Proof of the kill was a tongue broght back to the post.

As depicted in his wife's memoirs, published in 1889, General Custer confronts a buffalo after accidentally shooting his own mount.

165

create that new breed. From observation it appears that the cattalo has retained those characteristics of facing storms, pawing the snow for forage, eating snow when water is not available, and thriving on parched, scanty pastures. If we lose these characteristics the cattalo is not worth improving. Now that we are having a few fertile males, we are reorganizing the whole experiment. We plan to try to develop two strains of cattalo; one having approximately one-fourth buffalo blood, the other approximately one-eighth buffalo blood. Next to those two herds will be placed a herd of domestic cattle to be used as a check. Then the data and observations on all factors necessary to develop a beef breed will be collected. How long it will take, we do not know, but we hope to get something worthwhile. Furthermore, we do not intend to distribute any of this new stock until we are certain that they will be an improvement over the domestic cattle.

In the Far North, in the quadrangle limited by the Peace River, the Slave River, the Great Slave Lake, and the Caribou Mountains, a herd of buffalo lived and bred, almost untouched by the hectic massacre. Wild hay and native grasses were in profusion, there was an abundance of salt springs, and the sand hills made excellent wallowing grounds. The country was too rigorous for white men; and the Indians of the region lived chiefly on fish, which was easier to get than buffalo or moose. At the beginning of 1889, there must have been six hundred buffalo in this herd; there were not many wild buffalo throughout the western states.

The Canadian Government placed a permanent closed season on these buffalo, and entrusted the Northwest Mounted Police with their protection. By an Order-in-Council in 1922, 10,500 square miles of the Slave River District, embracing the buffalo range, were set aside for all time. Experienced rangers in cabins throughout the district guard this pledge Canada has made to nature.

The interest of the Canadian Government in the buffalo began as early as 1897, when a private gentleman presented three buffalo to the Rocky Mountains Park. In a generous enclosure at Banff, these buffalo (and one other, the gift of Lord Strathcona in 1898) so

Island in Alberta, Canada, is a refuge for many forms of ngered wildlife. Here, a young bull grazes in tranquility.

multiplied under their tender's close attention and careful crossing that twelve years later the herd numbered over one hundred.

One large buffalo refuge is located in Moiese, Montana, forty-seven miles north of Missoula. It can be reached by going north on U. S. 93 out of Missoula, then turning west at Ravalli on U. S. 10-A to its intersection with Montana secondary highway 212 near Dixon. From this point, the refuge headquarters lies about five miles due north.

The men of the wildlife service have a deep respect for the bison. They, like most Americans, refer to them as "buffalo." Actually, the bison is only a remote cousin of the true buffalo, which is the principal farm animal and beast of burden in Asia and Africa. And, it is remote indeed from Africa's cap buffalo, reputed to be the most dangerous animal on the globe.

There are many private herds around the West, ranging from ten to fifteen hundred buffalo, and the refuge animals are used to propagate them. Many bison are sold to owners of these private herds on the basis of a sealed competitive bid. In 1967, fifty-five were sold alive for an average of $412 each.

Those buffalo not sold to private herds are returned to the range for another year of grazing—except for a few that are butchered. Bison meat is sold to nonprofit clubs and organizations on a drawing basis. Last year's price was $120 per half-carcass.

Besides bison, the refuge range is also "home" to herds of elk, white-tailed and mule deer, bighorned sheep, pronghorn antelope, and some Texas Longhorn cattle. The refuge maintains an attractive exhibition area of varied range animals for summer tourists.

For the wildlife lover, however, the yearly October roundup offers the best opportunity to appreciate this magnificent native American animal—and the farsighted management of the Federal Government has helped bring it back from near oblivion.

Only twenty wild buffalo were left on the Moiese range when the refuge was founded in 1908. Today, thanks to the Montana refuge and others like it, there are more than ten thousand buffalo "back on the range." At Moiese's annual roundup, it is easy to visualize the herds as they once were.

It is even possible to purchase a buffalo calf alive and certified as to its good health; man finally took the necessary steps to preserve this unique American animal.

At the National Bison Range in Moiese, Montana, a large herd of bison leave the stream for the night.

The buffalo played his important part in the opening of the West: Without him, railroads would have gone bankrupt, homesteaders would have starved, and perhaps Indians would still roam the Great Plains of our western states. The buffalo, with his shaggy hair and hump, is a symbol of the growth of the United States. We, like the Indians, should consider him with awe and respect.

The vision persists, the labor goes on. The old tangible frontiers have vanished, but countless new ones, less tangible, have risen to take their place. We hope that the saga of the buffalo—The Blizzard's Children—will help to save for us, our children, and theirs, too, the endangered species of today. We cannot imagine a world without them.

Mandan women of the White Buffalo Cow Society, as drawn by Carl Bodmer.

Recommended Reading

Branch, E. Douglas. *The Hunting of the Buffalo*. New York, D. Appleton and Company, 1929.

Cody, Louisa. *Memories of Buffalo Bill*. New York and London, D. Appleton and Company, 1919.

Cook, James H. *Fifty Years on the Old Frontier*. New Haven, Yale University Press, 1923. New edition, Norman, University of Oklahoma Press, 1957.

Dixon, Olive K. *Life of Billy Dixon*. Dallas, P. L. Turner Company, 1927; Dallas, Southwest Press, 1927.

Ellsworth, Henry Leavitt. *Washington Irving on the Prairie*. Edited by Stanley T. Williams and Barbara D. Simison. New York, American Book Company, 1957.

Gard, Wayne. *The Great Buffalo Hunt*. New York, Alfred A. Knopf, 1959.

Grinnell, George Bird. *The Fighting Cheyennes*. New York, Charles Scribner's Sons, 1915. New edition, Norman, University of Oklahoma Press, 1956.

Haines, Francis. *The Buffalo*. New York, Thomas Y. Crowell Company, 1970.

Lavender, David. *Bent's Fort*. New York, Doubleday & Company, 1954.

McCreight, M. I. *Buffalo Bone Days*. Stykesville, Pennsylvania, Nupp Printing Company, 1939.

O'Conner, Richard. *Bat Masterson*. New York, Doubleday and Company, 1957.

Rister, Carl Coke. *Fort Griffin on the Texas Frontier*. Norman, University of Oklahoma Press, 1956.

Ruxton, George Frederick. *Life in the Far West*. Edited by LeRoy R. Hafen. Norman, University of Oklahoma Press, 1951.

Sandoz, Mari. *The Buffalo Hunters*. New York, Hastings House, 1954.

Vestal, Stanley. *Queen of the Cowtowns: Dodge City*. New York, Harper and Brothers, 1952.

Wallace, Ernest and E. Adamson Hoebel. *The Comanches: Lords of the South Plains*. Norman, University of Oklahoma Press, 1952.

Hide outfit compressing robes for shipment; HARPER'S MONTHLY, *1869.*

Index

Index

179

U

Y

W

Z

Acknowledgments

Acknowledgments